Language
Arts

Grade 6

FlashKids™

Flash Kids
A Division of Barnes & Noble
122 Fifth Avenue
New York, NY 10011

Dear Parent,

This book was developed to help your child improve the language skills he or she needs to succeed. The book emphasizes skills in the key areas of:

- grammar
- punctuation
- vocabulary
- writing
- research

The more than 100 lessons included in the book provide many opportunities for your child to practice and apply important language and writing skills. These skills will help your child improve his or her communication abilities, excel in all academic areas, and increase his or her scores on standardized tests.

About the Book

The book is divided into six units:

- Parts of Speech
- Sentences
- Mechanics
- Vocabulary and Usage
- Writing
- Research Skills

Your child can work through each unit of the book, or you can pinpoint areas for extra practice.

Lessons have specific instructions and examples and are designed for your child to complete independently. Grammar lessons range from using nouns and verbs to constructing better sentences. Writing exercises range from the friendly letter to the research report. With this practice, your child will gain extra confidence as he or she works on daily school lessons or standardized tests.

A thorough answer key is also provided so you may check the quality of answers.

A Step toward Success

Practice may not always make perfect, but it is certainly a step in the right direction. The activities in this book are an excellent way to ensure greater success for your child.

Table of Contents

Nouns

A **noun** is a word that names a person, place, thing, or an idea.
Examples:
boy, Juan, river, Texas, house, beach, joy

DIRECTIONS ▶ List the nouns from the sentences. Label each noun *person, place, thing,* or *idea.*

1. Carlos spent a week visiting his aunt and uncle.

   _____

2. Their daughter, Mary, is his favorite cousin.

   _____

3. The two children had long discussions about happiness.

   _____

4. The family lives on a ranch in Montana.

   _____

5. On Saturday my neighbor cooked a delicious meal.

   _____

6. Grandma helped clear the dishes from the table.

   _____

7. Sam did not leave the kitchen until the dishes were clean.

   _____

8. This month we will honor the memory of veterans of our town.

   _____

9. Volunteers will paint a mural at our school.

   _____

10. Dr. García, the mayor, will lead a parade with marching bands.

    _____

11. The lifeguard works two days a week.

    _____

12. Lightning struck the new barn.

    _____

Common Nouns and Proper Nouns

There are two main types of nouns: **common nouns** and **proper nouns.**
A **common noun** names any person, place, thing, or idea.
Examples:

 pilot, city, park

A **proper noun** names a particular person, place, or thing.
A proper noun begins with a capital letter.
Examples:

 Amelia Earhart, Chicago, Katmai National Park

DIRECTIONS ➤ **Rewrite the sentences correctly. Capitalize each proper noun and underline each common noun.**

1. Harriet tubman was born as a slave in the state of maryland.

   _____

2. Her husband, john tubman, was free.

   _____

3. Harriet fled from the plantation of her master.

   _____

4. The former slave found freedom in philadelphia.

   _____

5. Her family and friends were still enslaved.

   _____

6. This courageous woman returned for her sister, mary ann.

   _____

7. Her brother, james, escaped later with his family.

   _____

8. During her life, harriet led many other escapes.

   _____

Common and Proper Nouns, page 2

DIRECTIONS > Underline each common noun.

1. Monet was the first painter of the school of painting called Impressionism.

2. The name of this new style came from a painting by Monet called *Impression*: *Sunrise*.

3. The movement began in nineteenth-century France.

4. Monet was joined by thirty-nine other artists.

5. Those painters included Pierre-Auguste Renoir, Edgar Degas, and Paul Cézanne.

6. The first exhibit of paintings by this group was in Paris in April 1874.

7. The Impressionists wanted to capture on canvas how the eye saw light.

8. These painters were concerned with the way objects reflect light.

9. Monet often painted from a boat on the Seine River.

10. The painter died on December 5, 1926.

11. Children around the world play hopscotch.

12. There are many versions of the game.

13. In my town, Plainview, New York, children draw a board with eight squares.

14. They throw a stone or a coin into a square, hop on one foot into each square, and then return.

15. Can you write a paragraph about a sport that you like to play?

DIRECTIONS > Underline each proper noun.

16. Diego Rivera was one of the greatest painters and muralists of Mexico.

17. Because he loved Mexico, his works often portray the culture and history of that country.

18. One of his paintings reflects the time before the Spanish conquered Mexico.

19. That painting shows the Zapotec Indians making gold jewelry.

20. Although Rivera did some of his most famous murals in Mexico City, several of his works were painted in the United States.

21. Visit the Detroit Institute of Arts in Michigan to see some of the best works by Diego Rivera.

22. The Constitution of the United States was drafted at the Constitutional Convention.

23. Leaders from around the country met in Philadelphia, Pennsylvania.

24. The Bill of Rights was written by James Madison.

25. On April 30, 1789, George Washington took office as the leader of the country.

Common and Proper Nouns, page 3

DIRECTIONS Read the following sentences. Draw one line under each common noun. Circle each proper noun.

The four generals met beside the river. General Tang raised his violin and began playing a sad tune.

"Oh, I cannot bear to feel such sorrow," said General Wang. So Tang played a bright, happy song.

"How wonderful!" exclaimed General Lang. "That melody fills me with joy!"

"Yes," agreed General Mang. "But we have not come to this place to hear songs. We have come to discuss the future of our country. How can we be certain that this peace will last?"

DIRECTIONS Write common or proper nouns to complete the webs below. Use nouns from the paragraphs above. Then add two more nouns to each web.

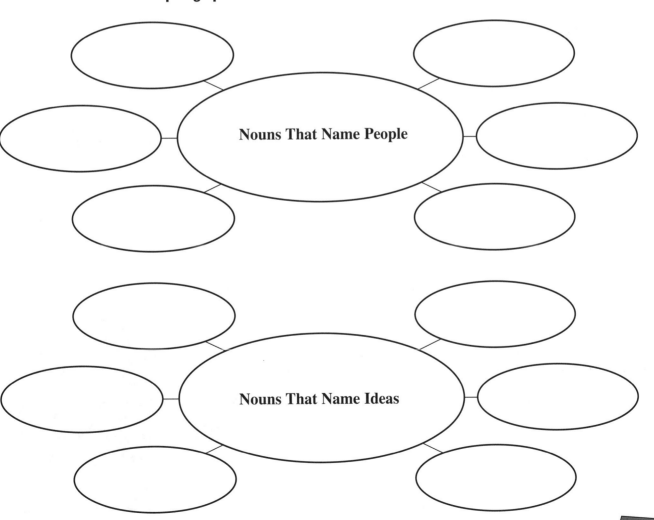

Nouns That Name People

Nouns That Name Ideas

Singular and Plural Nouns

A **singular noun** names one person, place, or thing.
Examples:
> principal, cafeteria, stereo

A **plural noun** names more than one person, place, or thing.
Examples:
> principals, cafeterias, stereos

Add *s* to most nouns to make them plural.
Examples:
> principal, principals   building, buildings

Add *es* to most nouns ending in *ch, sh, s,* or *x* to make them plural.
Examples:
> switch, switches   wish, wishes   box, boxes

If a noun ends in a consonant and *y,* change the *y* to *i* and add *es.*
Examples:
> community, communities   party, parties

If a noun ends in a vowel and *y,* add *s* to make it plural.
Examples:
> toy, toys   play, plays

DIRECTIONS ▸ **Complete each sentence, using the plural form of the noun in parentheses.**

1. Sally's family has _____.
   (horse)

2. They have _____, too.
   (donkey)

3. Sally's favorite horse is white with _____ of brown.
   (patch)

4. She always goes riding on clear _____.
   (day)

5. Her _____ like to trot along behind the horse.
   (puppy)

6. She waves to neighbors on their _____.
   (porch)

7. Several _____ like to ride with her.
   (lady)

8. They never wear _____ for riding.
   (dress)

9. Sally likes to ride over the _____.
   (hill)

10. She gallops on the _____.
    (trail)

Singular and Plural Nouns, page 2

Some nouns ending in *f* or *fe* are made plural by changing the *f* or *fe* to *ves*.
Examples:
> leaf, leaves   wife, wives

Some nouns ending in *f* are made plural by adding *s*.
Examples:
> roof, roofs   chief, chiefs

Most nouns ending in *o* that have a vowel just before the *o* are made plural by adding *s*.
Examples:
> radio, radios   stereo, stereos

Some nouns ending in *o* preceded by a consonant are made plural by adding *es*, but others are made plural by adding only *s*.
Examples:
> potato, potatoes   piano, pianos

A few nouns have irregular plural forms.
Examples:
> foot, feet   mouse, mice

A few nouns have the same form for both the singular and the plural.
Examples:
> sheep, sheep   trout, trout

DIRECTIONS ▸ **Complete each sentence, using the plural form of the noun in parentheses.**

1. Two _____ live on a farm in Alaska.
   (woman)

2. _____ cannot drive on the road by themselves.
   (Car)

3. The _____ on the farm have had _____.
   (ox)   (calf)

4. The farmers also raise _____.
   (sheep)

5. _____ sometimes try to attack them.
   (Wolf)

6. A wolf's _____ are as sharp as _____.
   (tooth)   (knife)

7. Some of the land is used to grow _____.
   (potato)

8. The farmers grow _____ during the summer.
   (tomato)

9. _____ eat the _____ of the plants.
   (Deer)   (leaf)

Singular and Plural Nouns, page 3

DIRECTIONS → Write the plural form for each singular noun and the singular form for each plural noun.

1. brush

_____

2. lice

_____

3. butterflies

_____

4. man

_____

5. suitcases

_____

6. turkey

_____

7. watches

_____

8. melody

_____

9. cheeses

_____

10. gases

_____

11. cranberry

_____

12. scarf

_____

13. hero

_____

14. ax

_____

15. blueberries

_____

16. geese

_____

17. mouth

_____

18. reef

_____

19. canary

_____

20. glitches

_____

21. umbrellas

_____

22. wells

_____

23. vase

_____

24. mosses

_____

25. lance

_____

26. mass

_____

27. patch

_____

28. video

_____

29. baby

_____

30. gulch

_____

31. cello

_____

32. sash

_____

Possessive Nouns

A **possessive noun** shows ownership or possession.

A **singular possessive noun** shows ownership by one person or thing. To form the possessive of most singular nouns, add an apostrophe (') and s.

Examples:

     my aunt's house   the tree's limbs

A **plural possessive noun** shows ownership by more than one person or thing. To form the possessive of a plural noun that ends in s, add an apostrophe (').

Examples:

     my friends' parents   the teachers' classes

To form the possessive of a plural noun that does not end in s, add an apostrophe (') and s.

Examples:

     the men's shoes   the mice's cheese

DIRECTIONS ▷ Rewrite each phrase using a possessive noun.

1. the book by Lewis Carroll _____

2. the edge of the knife _____

3. the cover of the book _____

4. the speech given by Mayor Sanita _____

5. the aroma of the flowers _____

6. the bicycle that belongs to the children _____

7. the roar of the sirens _____

8. the colors of the rainbow _____

9. the shoes that Chris owns _____

10. the purses that belong to the women _____

DIRECTIONS ▷ Write a possessive noun to complete each sentence.

11. I saw the _____ smile.

12. The _____ spots will not come off.

13. My _____ stories always make me laugh.

14. At midnight, you can see the _____ glow.

15. _____ illustrations are amazing.

Possessive Nouns, page 2

DIRECTIONS ▶ Write the singular possessive form of each noun.

1. sculptor _____
2. artist _____
3. hour _____
4. country _____
5. thief _____
6. Robert Frost _____
7. week _____
8. minute _____

9. weaver _____
10. Samuel Clemens _____
11. wolf _____
12. nurse _____
13. King Henry _____
14. moment _____
15. secretary _____
16. Mr. Jones _____

DIRECTIONS ▶ Write the plural possessive form of each noun.

17. hostesses _____
18. teachers _____
19. women _____
20. masters _____
21. workers _____
22. hours _____

23. oxen _____
24. spies _____
25. buffaloes _____
26. surgeons _____
27. sheep _____
28. secretaries _____

DIRECTIONS ▶ Rewrite each sentence. Use a possessive noun for part of the underlined phrase.

29. Charles Green was the worst balloonist in Britain.

_____

30. With the help of a colleague, he prepared for flight.

_____

31. Suddenly, the ropes of the balloon slipped off.

_____

32. How surprised the onlookers must have been to hear the calls for help from the flyers!

_____

Possessive Nouns, page 3

DIRECTIONS ➤ Write the possessive form of each noun in parentheses. Then label the possessive noun *singular* or *plural*.

1. (Luis) family celebrated Christmas together.

   _____

2. The (children) grandmother had the celebration at her ranch.

   _____

3. Their (parents) car was loaded with gifts.

   _____

4. They drove past the (sheep) pens on the way to the house.

   _____

5. They saw that the lettuce had become two (deer) dinner.

   _____

6. They could see their (cousins) faces through the window.

   _____

7. Each (person) gift from Grandmother was a sweater.

   _____

8. The (adults) sweaters were larger than the (children).

   _____

9. A turkey from the (Wilsons) ranch was the main course.

   _____

10. (Uncle Bernie) stuffing was a success as usual.

    _____

11. That night we went to the (neighbor) house to sing Christmas carols.

    _____

12. This was our (families) best Christmas ever!

    _____

Pronouns

A **pronoun** takes the place of one or more than one noun.
Examples:
   I, you, he, she, it, we, they

DIRECTIONS Write the pronoun from each sentence. Then write the noun that each pronoun refers to.

1. Some stories are designed to teach lessons; they are called fables.

_____

2. Aesop, a Greek slave, died more than two thousand years ago, but his fables are still famous.

_____

3. The slave told stories because he wanted to teach lessons.

_____

4. A story about a discontented donkey was first told by Aesop; it is one of Aesop's best fables.

_____

5. This fable is about a donkey and its owner.

_____

6. The owner had a dog she treated well.

_____

DIRECTIONS Rewrite each sentence, replacing appropriate nouns with pronouns.

7. The owner gave the dog a soft bed and fed the dog well.

_____

8. The donkey tried to make the donkey's owner treat the donkey well.

_____

9. The donkey learned that the donkey should not try to be something else.

_____

10. Can you write two fables and illustrate the fables?

_____

11. The chief engineer and the chief engineer's team watched.

_____

12. Moses took a kite and attached a rope to the kite.

_____

Agreement of Pronouns with Antecedents

When using a pronoun, make sure its **antecedent**, the noun to which it refers, is clear.
Example:
    Nicolás heard.   *He* heard.
Pronouns should agree with their antecedents in **number** and **gender**. Number tells whether a pronoun is singular or plural. Gender tells whether a pronoun is masculine, feminine, or neutral.
Example:
    Nicolás heard *a librarian* tell *stories.*
    He heard *her* tell *them.*
In the above example, *He* is singular and masculine, *her* is singular and feminine, and *them* is plural and neutral.

DIRECTIONS Write each pronoun. Then write its antecedent.

1. Thurgood Marshall was born in Maryland; his grandfather had been taken to Maryland as a slave.

   _____

2. Marshall's parents wanted to give their son a good education.

   _____

3. Marshall's mother was a teacher in the school her son attended.

   _____

4. Marshall decided that he wanted to be a lawyer.

   _____

5. Marshall attended Howard University Law School. It accepted black students when many other schools did not.

   _____

DIRECTIONS Write the pronoun in parentheses that correctly completes each sentence.

6. Marshall's mother sold _____ engagement ring to help pay for law school.
   (his, her)

7. Marshall was grateful to _____.
   (him, her)

8. Marshall later graduated first in _____ class.
   (his, their)

9. President Johnson appointed _____ to the Supreme Court.
   (him, them)

10. When people disagree with a court decision, _____ appeal to the
    (they, it)
    Supreme Court.

Subject and Object Pronouns

A **subject pronoun** is used as the subject or as part of the subject of a sentence. The subject pronouns are *I, you, he, she, it, we,* and *they.*
Example:
> *We* are ready to go.

An **object pronoun** is used as a direct or indirect object in a sentence. It can also be used after a preposition. The object pronouns are *me, you, him, her, it, us,* and *them.*
Example:
> Rebecca gave *me* a gift.   Rebecca gave the gift to *him.*

DIRECTIONS Complete each sentence by circling the correct pronoun in parentheses. Then write *subject pronoun* or *object pronoun* to identify the form you used.

1. Aunt Alicia gave (we, us) a book about Elizabeth Blackwell.

   _____

2. Elizabeth Blackwell's life story was fascinating to Lisa and (I, me).

   _____

3. (She, Her) and her sister became doctors.

   _____

4. (She, Her) was the first woman in the United States to enter medical school.

   _____

5. Other people disapproved of (she, her).

   _____

6. According to Daniel, (we, us) have many more opportunities than the girls did in Blackwell's day.

   _____

7. (He, Him) and his brother will have the same opportunities that women have.

   _____

8. Women like Elizabeth Blackwell have helped (we, us) by their example.

   _____

9. I admire (she, her) and her sister.

   _____

10. My father always tells (I, me) that I can become anything I want to be if I work hard.

    _____

11. I believe (he, him).

    _____

12. Can (you, him) reach for the stars?

    _____

13. Patricia and (I, me) will sing for you.

    _____

14. (They, Them) are ready to play soccer.

    _____

15. Bring (he, him) some paper and a pencil.

    _____

Subject and Object Pronouns, page 2

DIRECTIONS > Write the pronoun in parentheses that correctly completes each sentence.

1. My friends and _____ wish Anna Pavlova were still alive and dancing.
   (I, me)

2. _____ ballet fans consider her one of the greatest dancers of all time.
   (We, Us)

3. Anna's parents took _____ to a ballet.
   (she, her)

4. _____ encouraged their daughter to dance.
   (They, Them)

5. Anna later made _____ very proud.
   (they, them)

6. Anna met the great dancer Vaslav Nijinsky and danced with _____.
   (he, him)

7. I am sure _____ made a wonderful dancing couple.
   (they, them)

8. I wish I could have seen _____ dance.
   (they, them)

9. Perhaps _____ too will become a great dancer someday.
   (I, me)

10. _____ had a strange experience.
    (We, Us)

11. How did _____ get here?
    (I, me)

12. _____ were staring at the television.
    (They, Them)

13. Tell _____ what that is.
    (he, him)

14. People sang and danced for _____ all the time.
    (she, her)

15. Everyone was staring at _____.
    (they, them)

DIRECTIONS > Find two pronouns you did not use in the exercise above. Use each pronoun in a sentence.

_____

_____

_____

_____

Possessive Pronouns

A **possessive pronoun** shows ownership or possession of something.
The possessive pronouns *my, your, his, her, its, our,* and *their* are used before nouns.
Example:

Jerome is learning about *his* ancestors.

The possessive pronouns *mine, yours, his, hers, ours,* and *theirs* stand alone.
Example:

The picture is *his*.   The books are *mine*.

DIRECTIONS ▶ Rewrite each sentence. Use possessive pronouns to make the sentence less wordy.

1. Annie Oakley was famous for the shooting ability of Annie Oakley.

   _____

2. Mr. Oakley let her use the gun that he owned.

   _____

3. Buffalo Bill made Annie a star in the show that he had.

   _____

4. Annie never missed the target for which she aimed.

   _____

5. Audiences could hardly believe the eyes that belonged to them.

   _____

6. Jeremy wants to use the stereo that belongs to you.

   _____

7. The dog devoured the food that it had.

   _____

8. The Reynas had the couch that they owned reupholstered.

   _____

9. I want to change the schedule that belongs to me.

   _____

10. The animals ran for the lives of the animals.

   _____

Possessive Pronouns, page 2

DIRECTIONS ➤ Complete each sentence with a possessive pronoun.

1. Residents of St. Petersburg, Russia, are proud of _____ city.

2. We traveled to St. Petersburg to visit _____ friends.

3. Boris took us to see some of the most beautiful sights in _____ native city.

4. Marie and I, together with _____ friends, took a boat down the canals of the city.

5. Boris pointed out palaces where some of Russia's great rulers had made _____ homes.

6. At night the sun still shed _____ light on the city.

7. On nights at home, Russians love to make tea; it is _____ favorite beverage.

8. Tea and apple cake is a favorite late-night snack of _____.

9. St. Petersburg is full of flea markets where merchants show off _____ wares.

10. The traders set up _____ stalls along Nevsky Prospekt.

11. Marie invited us on a trip to one of _____ favorite places, the Kirov Islands.

12. This place has a charm all _____ own.

13. During World War II, the citizens of St. Petersburg endured a 900-day siege of _____ city by the Germans.

14. We saw a man with a ribbon on _____ coat, showing that he was a veteran of that siege.

15. People who suffered through that period wear _____ ribbons proudly.

16. Snow, ice, hunger, and disease took _____ toll among the brave residents of St. Petersburg.

17. _____ name at the time was Leningrad, in honor of Lenin, a leader of the revolution of 1917.

Reflexive Pronouns

A **reflexive pronoun** usually refers to the subject of a sentence.
The reflexive pronouns are *myself, yourself, himself, herself, itself, ourselves, yourselves,* and *themselves.*
Example:

Marie found *herself* alone in the quiet forest.

DIRECTIONS ▸ Underline each reflexive pronoun. Write the subject to which it refers.

1. Diane shook the sand off herself.

_____

2. Ben dried himself with a towel.

_____

3. The members of the other team warmed themselves up by swimming laps.

_____

4. We discussed the race among ourselves.

_____

5. I needed to be by myself for a few minutes.

_____

6. Do you ever need to be by yourself?

_____

7. The dog dried itself off by rolling in the grass.

_____

8. Ed and Beverly made themselves a mushroom and sausage pizza.

_____

9. I chopped the bell peppers and the onions myself.

_____

10. Estella and I won a prize for ourselves.

_____

DIRECTIONS ▸ Complete each sentence with a reflexive pronoun that agrees with its subject.

11. Elaine's towel was not in the pile when she went to dry _____.

12. It was at the end of the bench by _____.

13. For a moment, Ben found _____ without a towel.

14. Be sure you dry _____ well.

15. We must protect _____ from the cold.

16. I suggest that all swimmers dress _____ quickly.

17. I know that I have to keep _____ warm.

18. We also have to keep _____ covered.

19. Try not to allow _____ to get a cold.

20. The girls scared _____ by telling scary stories.

Indefinite Pronouns

An **indefinite pronoun** is a pronoun that does not refer to a specific person, place, thing, or idea.

The indefinite pronouns are *everyone, everything, everybody, anybody, many, most, few, each, some, someone, all, nothing, nobody,* and *no one.*

Example:

> *Someone* is knocking at the door.

An indefinite pronoun can be singular or plural. Follow the rules for subject-verb agreement when using indefinite pronouns as subjects.

Examples:

> *Some* of the girls are absent.   *Everyone* is sick.

DIRECTIONS Write the indefinite pronoun from each sentence. Then write *singular* or *plural* to identify the indefinite pronoun.

1. Everyone seems to be leaving.

   _____

2. Some have to stay.

   _____

3. Everything needs to be picked up.

   _____

4. Is anybody volunteering?

   _____

5. I see that many of you want to leave.

   _____

DIRECTIONS Write the verb form in parentheses that correctly completes each sentence.

6. Most of you _____ been fairly neat.
   (has, have)

7. A few _____ problems for the rest.
   (creates, create)

8. If each of you _____, it will not take long to clean up the mess.
   (helps, help)

9. Someone _____ to carry the trash to the bins.
   (needs, need)

10. All of us _____ to go home.
    (want, wants)

11. Now, nothing _____ out of place.
    (is, are)

Who, Whom, Whose

Use **who** as a subject pronoun and **whom** as an object pronoun.
Example:

Who is not going?   To *whom* am I speaking?

Do not confuse the possessive pronoun *whose* with the contraction *who's*.
Example:

Whose books are these?   *Who's* that at the door?

DIRECTIONS ▷ Write *who* or *whom* to complete each sentence.

1. _____ will help decorate the gym for the costume party?

2. _____ did you call?

3. Do you know _____ is planning to attend?

4. With _____ are you going?

5. _____ are you going to pretend to be?

6. From _____ did you get that idea?

7. Do you think the others will know _____ you are?

8. _____ can pick up the refreshments?

9. From _____ do we get the money to pay for them?

10. _____ is going to be the costume judge?

DIRECTIONS ▷ Write *whose* or *who's* to complete each sentence.

11. _____ going to drive everyone?

12. _____ parents have a van?

13. _____ your favorite cartoon character?

14. _____ the boy in the Napoleon costume?

15. This mask is mine, but _____ mask is that?

16. _____ costume did you borrow?

17. _____ Bradley supposed to be?

18. _____ selecting the best costume?

19. I can't decide _____ costume should win.

20. The person _____ the winner will get a prize.

Using Pronouns

DIRECTIONS ➤ Underline the pronouns in each sentence.

1. Leon asked Anne to tell him about some of her favorite books.

2. "Okay," Anne told him.

3. She chose two books and opened them.

4. Here are a few of the biographies about women pioneers.

5. I could talk about one of them.

6. Leon told her to pick one.

7. He enjoyed it.

8. I have been reading about Marie Dorion.

9. When Marie accompanied the trappers to Oregon, they showed her great respect.

10. Marie loved Pierre Dorion and traveled with him.

11. One day Marie found herself alone in the quiet forest.

12. Marie Dorion untied the horse and loaded it with supplies.

13. As the three of them left, Marie Dorion made herself a promise—that she and her children would survive.

14. Nine days later, a snowstorm trapped her and the boys.

15. The Dorions kept themselves alive for 53 days.

16. The Walla Walla Indians found Marie Dorion; they rescued her and the boys.

17. Anna Taylor went to Niagara Falls, but she crossed it differently.

18. Witnesses watched with their mouths open.

19. Taylor squeezed herself into a barrel.

20. Was she the first person to survive a trip over Niagara Falls?

21. The Kung people use eggshells to store their water supply.

22. A Ndaka bride is carried to her wedding on a shaded platform; indeed, the day is almost entirely hers.

23. Monica told herself that she must drive slowly.

24. Monica's younger sister and brother were with her.

25. Bob said that he was hungry.

26. The children amused themselves by singing.

27. Cars pulled off the highway because it was icy.

28. Monica drove slowly, but she still lost control.

29. For a moment she found herself helpless.

30. Then she maneuvered the car and stopped it.

31. Marla and Darnell both told me the news, but I didn't believe them at first.

32. I asked Mr. O'Reilly, but he hadn't heard anything about it.

33. Then Trina ran in and said that she had seen the whole thing.

34. After Trina explained just what had happened, I thanked her as politely as I could.

35. Then I smiled secretly, just to myself, and hurried away.

Adjectives

An **adjective** is a word that modifies, or describes, a noun or a pronoun.
Example:

We saw *lazy* lions beneath a *shady* tree.

Adjectives tell *what kind, how many,* or *which one.*
Examples:

lazy lions, *three* adults, *that* tree

The adjectives *a*, *an*, and *the* are called **articles**.
Use *a* before a word that begins with a consonant sound.
Examples:

a lion, *a* tree

Use *an* before a word that begins with a vowel sound.
Examples:

an adventure, *an* older lioness

DIRECTIONS ▷ Write each adjective. Label it *article* or *describing*.

1. Russia is an enormous country.

_____

2. It has long, cold winters.

_____

3. Rich crops are grown in the black, fertile earth.

_____

4. Many of the farms have early harvests.

_____

5. The lion is a sociable creature.

_____

6. A lioness, calm but alert, watches over her smallest cub.

_____

7. Cubs learn important skills at an early age.

_____

8. Nightly hunts may provide rich feasts.

_____

Adjectives, page 2

DIRECTIONS Change the meaning and tone of each sentence by replacing the adjectives. Write each new sentence.

1. The empty countryside has a lonely feeling.

   _____

2. We had a dull, boring visit in the dreary forests of Russia.

   _____

3. We then returned to the lively, bustling cities of the United States.

   _____

DIRECTIONS Use adjectives and articles to complete these sentences.

4. When the _____ lion is on the prowl, other _____

   animals must be cautious.

5. _____ wildebeest or _____ antelope could become a

   _____ lion's dinner.

6. Then the pride of lions, _____ and _____, might settle

   in for a _____ nap.

DIRECTIONS Imagine that you are an archaeologist being interviewed about the ancient Egyptians and their way of life. Use adjectives to answer the reporter's questions.

7. What words describe their kingdoms?

   _____

8. What type of person do you think a king or queen had to be in ancient Egypt?

   _____

9. What words describe their clothing and jewelry?

   _____

10. How do you feel about your most recent discovery?

   _____

Proper Adjectives

A **proper adjective** is an adjective that is formed from a proper noun. A proper adjective always begins with a capital letter.
Examples:

Proper Noun	Proper Adjective
Africa	African
Scotland	Scottish

DIRECTIONS Write the proper adjective from each sentence. Then write the proper noun from which the proper adjective was formed.

1. The African nations were especially interesting.

   _____

2. We bought some beautiful Hungarian crystal.

   _____

3. The English language was spoken there.

   _____

4. Our Yugoslavian friend came with us on our trip around the world.

   _____

5. Joyce enjoyed the Italian paintings.

   _____

6. Ralph liked the visit to a Tibetan monastery.

   _____

7. I studied Islamic law at the university.

   _____

8. Ron purchased a postcard with a picture of Nefertiti, a beautiful Egyptian queen.

   _____

9. We purchased Japanese paper for origami.

   _____

10. The Mexican pottery was less expensive at the market.

    _____

DIRECTIONS Write a sentence using the proper adjective formed from each proper noun.

11. China (Chinese)

    _____

12. Spain (Spanish)

    _____

13. Armenia (Armenian)

    _____

14. Britain (British)

    _____

15. Texas (Texan)

    _____

This, That, These, Those

A **demonstrative adjective** tells which one. The words *this, that, these,* and *those* are demonstrative adjectives.
Example:
    This book has more illustrations than *those* magazines.

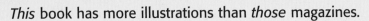

DIRECTIONS ▸ Write the demonstrative adjective from each sentence. Label the demonstrative adjective *singular* or *plural*.

1. This open house is going to be a real success.
   _____

2. Ask those students to come and help.
   _____

3. These science projects need to be arranged.
   _____

4. Where shall we display these drawings?
   _____

5. Put them on that bulletin board.
   _____

6. You must seize this opportunity.
   _____

DIRECTIONS ▸ Label each underlined word *adjective* or *pronoun*. Rewrite each sentence in which *this, that, these,* or *those* is used as a pronoun. Change the pronoun into a demonstrative adjective.

7. What shall I do with <u>these</u>?
   _____

8. Arrange them on <u>that</u> table.
   _____

9. Do we have any more of <u>those</u>?
   _____

10. Look in <u>this</u> drawer.
    _____

11. Did you draw <u>that</u>?
    _____

12. Are <u>those</u> maps clear?
    _____

13. Shall I look in <u>these</u>?
    _____

14. <u>That</u> table is covered with books and maps.
    _____

Predicate Adjectives

A **predicate adjective** is an adjective that follows a linking verb and describes the subject of a sentence. Forms of *be* are the most common linking verbs. Other linking verbs include forms of *taste, look, smell, feel, appear, seem,* and *become.*
Example: I look *tired*, but I feel *fine*.

DIRECTIONS Write the predicate adjective from each sentence. Then write the word it modifies.

1. The air feels warm today. _____

2. The flowers smell unusually sweet. _____

3. High in the sky is the sun. _____

4. The horses look peaceful in the meadow. _____

5. Sharon feels happy outside. _____

6. She is eager for a ride on her horse. _____

7. Her horse appears ready to go. _____

8. How beautiful is the day! _____

9. The surgeon was skillful in the operating room. _____

10. The mango tastes bitter, but I will eat it anyway. _____

11. That horse at the far end of the meadow is fast. _____

12. Its coat appears gray in the shade. _____

13. However, it becomes silver in the bright sun. _____

14. Horses like that are unusual. _____

15. They are usually well-trained. _____

16. Rin Tin Tin and Lassie seem brave in their movies. _____

17. When audiences watched, they felt good. _____

18. Rin Tin Tin looked fearless. _____

DIRECTIONS Use the linking verb to write a sentence containing a predicate adjective.

19. feel _____

20. taste _____

Comparison with Adjectives: *er, est*

An adjective has three degrees of comparison: **positive**, **comparative**, and **superlative**.
The *positive degree* of an adjective is used when no comparison is being made.
Example:
>   This is a *hot* day.

The *comparative degree* of an adjective is used to compare two items. Form the comparative of most one-syllable adjectives by adding *er*. For some words that end in consonants, double the consonant before you add *er*.
Example:
>   Today is *hotter* than yesterday.

The *superlative degree* of an adjective is used to compare three or more items. Form the superlative of most one-syllable adjectives by adding *est*. For some words that end in consonants, double the consonant before you add *est*.
Example:
>   This is the *hottest* day of the year.

DIRECTIONS ▶ Write the comparative form and the superlative form of each adjective.

Positive	Comparative	Superlative
1. cold	_____	_____
2. safe	_____	_____
3. funny	_____	_____
4. flat	_____	_____
5. shiny	_____	_____
6. tall	_____	_____
7. white	_____	_____
8. sweet	_____	_____
9. sad	_____	_____
10. young	_____	_____

DIRECTIONS ▶ Choose the form of the adjective in parentheses that correctly completes the sentence.

11. France is _____ than Luxembourg.
        (large)

12. Austria is _____ than France.
        (small)

13. Luxembourg is the _____ of the three countries.
        (small)

Other Comparisons

Use **more** or **less** and **most** or **least** to form the comparative and the superlative of most adjectives with two or more syllables.
Examples:

wonderful, more wonderful, most wonderful

wonderful, less wonderful, least wonderful

Some adjectives have special forms for comparing. Memorize adjectives that change spelling completely in the comparative and the superlative degrees.
Examples:

good, better, best

DIRECTIONS Write the comparative form and the superlative form of each adjective.

Positive	Comparative	Superlative
1. energetic		
2. difficult		
3. generous		
4. affectionate		
5. active		
6. bad		
7. much		
8. likely		
9. expensive		
10. crowded		

DIRECTIONS Rewrite each sentence. Use the form of the adjective in parentheses that correctly completes the sentence.

11. Ruffles is the (beautiful) puppy of the litter.

_____

12. Sport is (intelligent) than Ruffles.

_____

13. Of all the puppies, Tuffy is the (much) fun.

_____

Using Adjectives

DIRECTIONS ➤ Write the correct degree of comparison for the adjective in parentheses.

1. The stone houses of wealthy Mayas looked _____ (strong) and

   _____ (impressive) than those of their poorer neighbors.

2. The clothing of Mayan priests was the _____ (elaborate) of all.

3. The _____ (beautiful) city of Tenochtitlán may have been the Aztecs'

   _____ (great) achievement.

4. The Incas, who seem to have been _____ (aggressive) than the Aztecs or

   the Mayas, ruled the _____ (large) empire in the hemisphere.

5. We were all competing to see who could create the _____ (good) poster

   about an ancient civilization.

6. The Great Wall of China wasn't a _____ (bad) idea at all!

7. This poster is definitely _____ (good) than last year's winner.

8. Ms. Mata is feeling _____ (good) than she did yesterday, rather than

   _____ (bad), so she'll judge the posters this afternoon.

9. This contest has been _____ (much) fun than last year's contest.

10. In fact, it may be the _____ (good) activity of the year.

DIRECTIONS ➤ Underline the adjectives in each sentence below.

11. The fierce battle at Gettysburg took place in 1863.

12. This battle was not the first conflict of the Civil War.

13. Few Southerners reached Union lines.

14. A general named Robert E. Lee led the Confederate army.

15. The Confederates approached under heavy gunfire.

16. That army would not turn back during an attack.

17. Many soldiers on both sides were killed.

18. Gettysburg is a pivotal battle in American history.

19. President Lincoln visited the site several months later.

20. He read a memorable speech, now known as the Gettysburg Address.

◎ **33**

Action Verbs

An **action verb** tells what the subject of a sentence does or did.
Examples:

        She *sleeps* every day.   She *slept* yesterday.

DIRECTIONS ▶ Underline the action verb in each sentence.

1. Dr. James Naismith originated the game of basketball.

2. The Hillside team and the Seaside team compete every year.

3. The two centers leaped for the ball.

4. They stretched their arms high into the air.

5. A Hillside forward grabbed the ball.

6. The forward dribbled the ball to the end of the court.

7. She aimed for the basket.

8. The ball flew through the air.

9. The ball bounced off the backboard.

10. Several players jumped for the ball.

DIRECTIONS ▶ Rewrite each sentence. Use a strong action verb to make the sentence more vivid.

11. A Seaside forward got the ball.

_____

12. Her teammate went to the other end of the court.

_____

13. The forward sent the ball the length of the court.

_____

14. Romelia put the ball into the basket.

_____

15. The Seaside fans and players yelled excitedly.

_____

Linking Verbs

A **linking verb** connects the subject of a sentence to a noun that renames the subject or to an adjective that describes it.
The most common linking verb is *be*. Some forms of *be* are *am, is, are, was,* and *were.*
Example:

Carolyn *is* tired.

DIRECTIONS → Write the verb from each sentence. Label it *action* or *linking*.

1. The family celebrated Thanksgiving at Uncle Tómas's house.

   _____

2. His house is large enough for us all.

   _____

3. His table reaches from one end of the dining room to the other.

   _____

4. Uncle Tómas cooked the whole dinner by himself.

   _____

5. He appeared tired.

   _____

6. However, he greeted everyone with warmth and enthusiasm.

   _____

7. The turkey smelled wonderful.

   _____

8. Everyone became impatient.

   _____

9. The dinner table looked beautiful.

   _____

10. The greenhouse effect is a danger to our environment.

    _____

11. Heat rises.

    _____

12. Some heat energy escapes Earth's atmosphere.

    _____

13. Many gases are colorless and odorless.

    _____

14. High levels of carbon dioxide were present.

    _____

15. The Industrial Revolution was a turning point for the environment.

    _____

16. Many researchers study global warming.

    _____

17. Our community recycles glass, newspaper, and aluminum.

    _____

18. It was a terrific place.

    _____

19. Connie opened the big umbrella.

    _____

20. The king and queen were quite argumentative.

    _____

Action Verbs and Linking Verbs

DIRECTIONS Read the following passage. Then underline the action verbs and circle the linking verbs.

Marathoners are amazing athletes. They compete in races more than 26 miles long. The best marathoners are usually small and slight. They need very strong legs and powerful lungs, too. Youth, however, is not necessarily an advantage in a marathon.

This long race carries the name of an ancient battlefield. In 490 B.C., the Greeks defeated the Persians at Marathon. According to legend, a Greek soldier ran all the way from Marathon to Athens with news of the victory. He ran more than 20 miles. Now a marathon is a regular part of the Olympic Games. The official distance for an Olympic marathon is 42,195 meters, or 26 miles and 385 yards.

DIRECTIONS Complete the following sentences. Add the kind of verb identified in parentheses.

1. The team members _____ every day.
   (action)

2. Their coach _____ them.
   (action)

3. The day of the big race _____ .
   (action)

4. The athletes _____ enthusiastic.
   (linking)

5. They _____ .
   (action)

6. Coal, oil, and natural gas _____ fossil fuels.
   (linking)

7. Dr. Huong _____ global warming.
   (action)

8. Some students _____ a model of our planet.
   (action)

9. Wood _____ a renewable resource.
   (linking)

10. Technology _____ problems as well as solutions.
   (action)

Main Verbs and Helping Verbs

A verb phrase is made up of two or more verbs. The **main verb** is the most important verb in a verb phrase.
Example:

My teacher <u>was</u> *born* in Venezuela.

The last word of a verb phrase is the main verb. The other words are **helping verbs**.
Example:

My teacher <u>*was*</u> born in Venezuela.

DIRECTIONS ➤ Underline the verb phrase in each sentence, and circle the main verb.

1. The Powells are moving.

2. They have lived next door for ten years.

3. I am missing them already.

4. Their son has been my best friend for a long time.

5. The family had moved here from California.

6. Why do they want a different house?

7. Mrs. Powell has accepted a job in New York.

8. Her sister is living in New York.

9. She was working for a large publishing company.

10. The same company did offer Mrs. Powell a job.

11. Does she like big cities?

12. She was not complaining in her last letter.

13. She had lived in Chicago at one time.

14. She is enjoying the museums.

15. Mr. Powell will find a good job.

16. Their son has entered school.

17. He might meet many new friends.

18. A tai chi master may visit our school.

19. His daughter is living in the United States.

20. She could give us a lesson in tai chi.

Main Verbs and Helping Verbs, page 2

DIRECTIONS Write *main verb* or *helping verb* to identify the underlined verb in each sentence.

1. The tiny curtain <u>will</u> slowly open. _____

2. Two figures <u>are</u> dancing into view. _____

3. The figures are <u>called</u> puppets. _____

4. Puppets can be <u>made</u> out of cloth and wood. _____

5. Our puppet theater may <u>give</u> three shows a year. _____

6. Each show <u>is</u> performed for four weekends. _____

7. New plays are <u>rehearsed</u> carefully. _____

8. I <u>have</u> become a puppeteer with the company. _____

9. I <u>am</u> memorizing lines and movements. _____

10. The new play was <u>written</u> in Spanish and English. _____

11. Sometimes our lines are <u>spoken</u> in English. _____

12. Sometimes audiences <u>have</u> asked for Spanish. _____

13. All the puppeteers <u>can</u> speak both languages. _____

14. We <u>should</u> do this for several years. _____

15. <u>Do</u> the audiences enjoy the shows? _____

DIRECTIONS Complete these sentences with a main verb and a helping verb from the box.

are	were	does	need	should
will	be	blooming	picked	visit

16. The roses _____ _____ today.

17. The garden _____ _____ beautiful next year.

18. Everyone _____ _____ during the summer.

19. A sturdy sunflower _____ not _____ support.

20. The apples _____ already _____.

Principal Parts of Verbs

The **principal parts** of verbs are the **present, present participle, past,** and **past participle**.

For regular verbs, the present participle is formed by adding *ing* to the present. It is used with a form of the helping verb *be*.

The past and the past participle of regular verbs are formed by adding *ed* or *d* to the present. The past participle uses a form of the helping verb *have*.

Examples:

Present	Present Participle	Past	Past Participle
play	(is, are, am) playing	played	(have, has, had) played
move	(is, are, am) moving	moved	(have, has, had) moved

An irregular verb forms its past and past participle in other ways. A dictionary shows the principal parts of these verbs.

DIRECTIONS Underline the main verb in each sentence. Write *present, present participle, past,* or *past participle* to label the main verbs.

1. Randy's class studies world history. _____

2. The students are reading about the Renaissance. _____

3. The teacher has taught them about the art of that time. _____

4. They have learned much about Renaissance painting. _____

5. Yesterday they visited an art museum. _____

6. They had always gone to a different museum before. _____

7. They had seen a display of Egyptian art at the Egyptian Museum. _____

8. The English teachers had read two new novels. _____

9. The band director is planning the fall musical. _____

10. The cafeteria monitor talks to the children. _____

DIRECTIONS Write the correct form of the verb in parentheses in each sentence. At the end of each sentence, label the verb *present, present participle, past,* or *past participle.*

11. These days the class _____ something about history every week. (learn)

_____

12. Today the students are _____ a movie about Leonardo da Vinci. (watch)

_____

Principal Parts of Verbs, page 2

DIRECTIONS ▶ Write the present participle, past, and past participle of each verb.

Present	Present Participle (with *is, are, am*)	Past	Past Participle (with *have, has, had*)
1. hike	hiking	hiked	hiked
2. try			
3. show			
4. talk			
5. bring			
6. ring			
7. create			
8. fly			
9. drink			
10. witness			
11. wear			
12. catch			
13. grow			
14. begin			
15. go			
16. sit			
17. think			
18. see			
19. teach			
20. understand			
21. forget			
22. splash			
23. eat			
24. watch			
25. arrive			

Present, Past, and Future Tenses

The **tense** of a verb tells the time of the action or being.
Present tense tells that something is happening now.
Examples:

Dena *laughs* at the jokes.   Jon *walks* home.

Past tense tells that something happened in the past. The action is over.
Examples:

Dena *laughed* at the jokes.   Jon *walked* home.

Future tense tells that something will happen in the future. Use *will* with the verb.
Examples:

Dena *will laugh* at the jokes.   Jon *will walk* home.

DIRECTIONS ➤ Write the verb from each sentence and label it *present, past,* or *future.*

1. Marlene works in her garden every day.

   _____

2. Yesterday she prepared the ground for the tomatoes.

   _____

3. Tomorrow she will set the plants in the ground.

   _____

4. She planted carrots last week.

   _____

5. Leaves will appear in a few days.

   _____

6. Marlene will pick radishes tomorrow.

   _____

7. She pulls weeds every day.

   _____

8. The garden will soon be full of vegetables.

   _____

9. Teddy's team will bat first.

   _____

10. The visiting team always bats first.

    _____

11. In the last game, she played first base.

    _____

12. Sometimes a player changes positions.

    _____

13. The coach gives everyone a chance to play.

    _____

DIRECTIONS ➤ Write a sentence with each verb, using the tense in parentheses.

14. water (present) _____

15. dig (future) _____

16. grow (future) _____

17. help (past) _____

Perfect Tenses

There are three **perfect tenses: present perfect, past perfect**, and **future perfect**.
Form the perfect tenses with the past participle and the helping verbs *have, has, had,*
or *will have.*
Examples:

        Mr. Lee *has arranged* a comedy show for us. (present perfect)
        Mr. Lee *had arranged* a comedy show for us. (past perfect)
        Mr. Lee *will have arranged* a comedy show for us. (future perfect)

DIRECTIONS ▶ Underline the verb in each sentence and label it *present perfect, past perfect,*
or *future perfect.*

1. We have started a reading club.

   _____

2. By next year, we will have discussed eight books.

   _____

3. Susan often had suggested the book *Little Women* to the club members.

   _____

4. I have always enjoyed books by Louisa May Alcott.

   _____

5. I will have finished the book before the next meeting.

   _____

6. The school newspaper has written about our group.

   _____

7. The reporter had interviewed us last year.

   _____

8. We have chosen the book *The Secret Garden* as our next selection.

   _____

DIRECTIONS ▶ Complete each sentence, using the correct perfect tense of the verb in parentheses.

9. Tom _____ sitting next to Francie this year. (enjoy)

10. He _____ not _____ her before September. (meet)

11. Next week they _____ each other for six months. (know)

12. They _____ often _____ their favorite books this year. (share)

13. Francie read a novel because Tom _____ it. (recommend)

Irregular Verbs

An **irregular verb** does not end with *ed* to form the past and the past participle. Verbs such as *be, have*, and *do* form the past and the past participle in other ways.
Examples:

Present	Past	Past Participle
is, are, am	was	were
has, have	had	had
do, does	did	done

DIRECTIONS ▶ Complete each sentence with the correct form of the verb in parentheses.

1. I _____ excited about our camping trip.
    (am, is)

2. I _____ wanted to visit Yosemite for years.
    (has, have)

3. _____ you looking forward to it, too?
    (Is, Are)

4. _____ your family go camping often?
    (Does, Do)

5. Last year we _____ going camping once each month.
    (was, were)

6. We _____ planning to go camping every year.
    (is, are)

7. Jason _____ going to come camping with us.
    (was, were)

8. His parents _____ not letting him go camping.
    (is, are)

9. I _____ not think that is fair.
    (does, do)

10. We _____ purchased a lot of camping equipment.
    (has, have)

DIRECTIONS ▶ Use a form of *be, have*, or *do* to complete each sentence.

11. Yosemite Valley _____ carved by glaciers.

12. Glaciers _____ cut a mountain in half.

13. The mountain _____ called Half Dome.

14. _____ anyone ever climb Half Dome?

More Irregular Verbs

Remember that an **irregular verb** is a verb that does not end with *ed* to show the past and the past participle.
Examples:

I *ate* at home.   I *have eaten* at home.

DIRECTIONS Complete each sentence. Write the past or the past participle form of the verb in parentheses.

1. Nancy's peach tree has _____ several feet.
   (grow)

2. She _____ it five years ago.
   (buy)

3. Another gardener had _____ it to her.
   (sell)

4. Since then, she has _____ hours caring for it.
   (spend)

5. She has _____ very good care of it.
   (take)

6. It has _____ a very large tree.
   (become)

7. Her friends have never _____ such beautiful peaches.
   (see)

8. Nancy has _____ some peaches to them.
   (give)

9. Her family has already _____ a few this summer.
   (eat)

10. Last year she _____ several pounds of peaches.
    (freeze)

11. She _____ dozens of pies.
    (make)

12. This year she has _____ the bruised peaches for jam.
    (choose)

13. The neighbors have _____ Nancy how to make jam.
    (tell)

14. They also _____ a variety of vegetables in their garden.
    (grow)

15. Sarah and María have _____ fresh produce at the market.
    (buy)

Direct Objects

A **direct object** is the noun or pronoun that receives the action of the verb. A direct object tells who or what receives the action.
Example:
    Bobby loved his *parents*.

DIRECTIONS Underline the direct object in each sentence.

1. A narrow strip of land once connected North America with South America.

2. The strip of land blocked ocean travel between the Atlantic Ocean and the Pacific Ocean.

3. The Panama Canal now divides the two continents.

4. It provides a short route from the Atlantic Ocean to the Pacific Ocean.

5. The United States operated the canal after building it.

6. Before the eruption of Mount St. Helens, people heard a deep rumble.

7. People more than 200 miles away noticed the noise.

8. Hot gas and ash burned entire forests.

9. The eruption killed more than 60 people.

10. Many residents lost their homes.

11. My dog Chester eats tomatoes.

12. He devours potatoes.

13. My dog wrinkles the covers on the bed.

14. I flatten the pillows on the sofa.

15. Silvia takes a nap every afternoon.

DIRECTIONS Rewrite each incomplete sentence, adding a direct object.

16. Rough seas near Cape Horn endangered.

_____

17. Ships can carry from one ocean to another in far less time.

_____

18. A Panama Canal pilot guides through the Canal.

_____

19. The United States paid to Panama for control of the Canal.

_____

Indirect Objects

An **indirect object** tells to whom or for whom the action of the verb is done.
Example:
   Jack showed the *dog* kindness.

DIRECTIONS > Rewrite each sentence, using an indirect object.

1. Sheila told a secret to Don.

_____

2. Don gave his promise of silence to her.

_____

3. Mr. Miller was giving a surprise party for Ryan.

_____

4. He had sent an invitation to Sheila.

_____

5. Mrs. Miller handed an invitation to Don.

_____

6. Don asked a question of Mrs. Miller.

_____

DIRECTIONS > Underline the indirect object in each sentence.

7. The three pals gave their guests a hearty welcome.

8. I sent my friends holiday cards with pictures of the animals.

9. My friends asked me questions about the first meeting.

10. A TV talk show host gave us a spot on her program.

11. I told her the facts.

12. An animal-food company sent me boxes of free food.

13. A restaurant owner gave me a free meal.

14. The animals brought my family a lot of public attention.

15. My neighbors bought them new leashes.

16. The animals still gave everyone friendly greetings.

Predicate Nominatives

A **predicate nominative** is a noun or pronoun that follows a linking verb and renames the subject.
Example:
> Lassie has been a *celebrity* for decades.

DIRECTIONS ▸ Write the predicate nominative from each sentence.

1. Fred is an enthusiastic hiker. _____

2. He is a member of a hiking club. _____

3. Jill is his best friend. _____

4. She is the fastest walker in the club. _____

5. The president of the club is Michelle. _____

6. She is an energetic girl. _____

7. Her mother is a famous climber. _____

8. Mrs. Wu is the teacher of his art class now. _____

9. Oil painting is part of the class's training. _____

10. Enrique's first oil painting was a portrait of his mother. _____

11. Enrique will become a professional artist. _____

12. An obedience trial is a good test. _____

13. The person who observes your pet is the judge. _____

14. The pet show organizer was Estella. _____

15. The funniest entry in the show was a poodle. _____

DIRECTIONS ▸ Complete each sentence, using a predicate nominative that fits the description in parentheses.

16. It was _____.
    (day of the week)

17. The group was _____.
    (a club)

18. The leader of the hike was _____.
    (a girl)

19. The group's destination was _____.
    (a place)

Transitive and Intransitive Verbs

A **transitive verb** is an action verb that is followed by a noun or a pronoun that receives the action.
Example:
> I *know* the story.

An **intransitive verb** includes all linking verbs and any action verbs that do not take an object.
Example:
> My friends *cried*.

DIRECTIONS ➤ Underline the verb in each sentence. Label it *transitive* or *intransitive*.

1. The Mendozas went to the Grand Canyon.

2. They had never visited it before.

3. Mr. Mendoza drove the car most of the way.

4. He drove for miles through the desert.

5. The children rode in the back seat.

6. Luis saw the canyon first.

7. No one felt sadder than Roberto.

8. Roberto loved the shepherd!

9. The next day the caretaker did stop.

10. Bobby had found a home on the prairie.

11. The workers had built a sturdy metal fence.

12. I inherited a cat from the former tenants.

13. Smith, the cat, sat quietly on the sofa.

14. I drove to the kennel for my two dogs.

15. The dogs would see Smith soon.

16. I offered the dogs treats.

17. I gave each dog a warning about politeness.

18. Then I entered the house with the two canines.

19. The cat bristled.

20. I gave the cat a hug.

21. The poodle gave the cat a sniff.

22. Jones understood cats.

Adverbs

> An **adverb** modifies a verb, an adjective, or another adverb.
> An adverb tells *how, when, where,* or *to what extent.*
> *Examples:*
>
> Our skates moved *effortlessly*. (how)
> The ice is glistening *now*. (when)
> The canals are frozen *there*. (where)
> The air was *very* dry. (to what extent)

DIRECTIONS ➤ Write the adverb from each sentence. Label the adverb *how, when, where,* or *to what extent.*

1. Kevin rose early and watched the sun rise. _____

2. He looked up and saw billowing clouds. _____

3. They were very beautiful in the soft light. _____

4. A large gray hawk circled lazily. _____

5. A gopher cautiously poked its nose out of its hole. _____

6. Hans dressed warmly. _____

7. He walked outside. _____

8. He waved happily to his friends. _____

9. The air was quite cold. _____

10. Many people skated tonight. _____

DIRECTIONS ➤ Write each adverb and the word it modifies. Label the modified word *verb, adjective,* or *adverb.*

11. Kevin watched the gopher very quietly. _____

12. He remained quite still. _____

13. The world gradually awoke. _____

14. Singing birds sweetly greeted the morning. _____

15. Kevin heard his parents' voices and returned reluctantly. _____

16. He suddenly felt very hungry. _____

Placement of Adverbs in Sentences

Place most adverbs that modify adjectives or other adverbs just before the word they modify.

Examples:

Clouds scudded *very* swiftly across the sky.

The sky was *quite* beautiful.

Place most adverbs that modify verbs almost anywhere in the sentence.

Examples:

Lifeguards watched the swimmers *carefully*.

Lifeguards *carefully* watched the swimmers.

DIRECTIONS ▶ Write the adverbs from the sentences. Label each one *yes* if it can be moved or *no* if it cannot be moved.

1. Very rough surf discouraged most of the sailors. _____

2. Bruce can be rather careless. _____

3. Recklessly, Bruce sailed out of the harbor. _____

4. Suddenly, the wind rose. _____

5. He struggled desperately with the sails. _____

6. The largest crowds appeared later. _____

7. A strong undertow could be quite dangerous. _____

8. Our lifeguard warned a swimmer sternly. _____

9. Smart swimmers always observe the rules. _____

10. The sand grew quite hot under the blazing sun. _____

DIRECTIONS ▶ Add the adverb in parentheses to each sentence and write the sentence. Vary placement of the adverbs.

11. A wave crashed over Bruce's boat. (heavily)

_____

12. The boat overturned in the water. (clumsily)

_____

13. Bruce floundered in the water. (helplessly)

_____

14. Another boat observed Bruce's struggle. (immediately)

_____

Comparison with Adverbs

To form the **comparative** or the **superlative** of most short adverbs, add *er* or *est*.
Example:

Bradley is *nicer* than his brother.

Use *more* or *less* and *most* or *least* instead of *er* and *est* with adverbs that end in *ly* or have two or more syllables.
Example:

Today is the *most enjoyable* day I have had all year.

DIRECTIONS Write the comparative form and the superlative form of each adverb.

1. low _____ _____

2. near _____ _____

3. slowly _____ _____

4. seriously _____ _____

5. eagerly _____ _____

6. fast _____ _____

7. frequently _____ _____

8. readily _____ _____

9. noticeably _____ _____

10. easy _____ _____

DIRECTIONS Complete each sentence. Use the correct form of the adverb in parentheses.

11. Leslie and Patrick practice archery _____ than Ron and Janet do.
    (often)

12. Leslie scored _____ of all the students in the class.
    (high)

13. She aimed _____ than the others.
    (carefully)

14. Patrick was surprised when she shot _____ than he did.
    (accurately)

15. He is strong, and his arrows always fly _____ than hers.
    (far)

16. _____ than last time, he raised his bow.
    (slowly)

Negatives

Negatives are words that mean "no." The words *no, not, never, nowhere, nothing, nobody, no one, neither, scarcely*, and *barely* are common negatives. Use only one negative in a sentence.

Example:

CORRECT   No one should ever drive on ice.
INCORRECT No one should never drive on ice.

DIRECTIONS ➤ **Write the word in parentheses that correctly completes each negative sentence.**

1. On one side of the planet Mercury, the sun does not _____ set.
   (ever, never)

2. The other side of the planet gets _____ sun at all.
   (no, any)

3. _____ on this planet are the temperatures moderate.
   (Anywhere, Nowhere)

4. As far as we know, Mercury has _____ moons.
   (any, no)

5. There is not _____ who has been to Mercury.
   (anybody, nobody)

6. We do not know _____ about Mercury.
   (everything, nothing)

7. _____ of us can fly there.
   (Neither, Either)

DIRECTIONS ➤ **Choose three statements from the activity above. Rewrite each negative statement using the word you did not choose from the parentheses. You will need to change other words to write the sentences correctly.**

8. _____

   _____

9. _____

   _____

10. _____

    _____

Adverb or Adjective?

Remember that most words ending in *ly* are adverbs.
Example:
> Weather changes *quickly*.

Use *good* only as an adjective.
Example:
> The play was *good*.

Use *well* as an adjective to mean "healthy" and as an adverb to tell how something is done.
Examples:
> Linda is doing *well* after her surgery.   The surgery went *well*.

DIRECTIONS ▶ Write the word in parentheses that completes each sentence correctly.

1. King Edward was _____ ill.
   (serious, seriously)

2. He did not become _____ and finally he died.
   (good, well)

3. His relative, William, was _____ determined to have the throne.
   (real, really)

4. Edward had promised it to him _____ before he died.
   (short, shortly)

5. The English nobles made Prince Harold king _____ after Edward's death.
   (immediate, immediately)

6. William _____ refused to accept their decision.
   (stubborn, stubbornly)

7. He _____ raised an army.
   (quick, quickly)

8. The army attacked _____.
   (fierce, fiercely)

9. Harold fought _____, but he was killed.
   (brave, bravely)

10. William the Conqueror was a _____ fighter.
    (good, well)

11. He was a _____ leader.
    (powerful, powerfully)

12. His subjects were required to obey him _____.
    (perfect, perfectly)

13. He punished disobedience _____.
    (cruel, cruelly)

Prepositions and Prepositional Phrases

A **preposition** shows the relationship of a noun or a pronoun to another word in the sentence.

Example:

I walked *along* the beach.

The **object of the preposition** is the noun or the pronoun that follows the preposition.

Example:

The sands of the *beach* were white.

A **prepositional phrase** is made up of a preposition, the object of the preposition, and all the words in between.

Example:

Who lives *in that house*?

DIRECTIONS ▷ Write the prepositional phrase from each sentence. Then underline the preposition. Circle the object of the preposition.

1. Marco Polo's family left Venice in 1271. _____

2. They took young Marco with them. _____

3. China lay far beyond the eastern mountains. _____

4. The Polos traveled all the way to China. _____

5. They stayed there for many years. _____

6. Marco returned from China twenty-five years later. _____

7. Marco Polo wrote a book about it. _____

8. He had traveled extensively through Asia. _____

9. The book described Marco's travels for his readers. _____

10. Europeans learned about Asia from Marco Polo's book. _____

DIRECTIONS ▷ Underline the prepositional phrase or phrases in each sentence.

11. Many passengers leaned over the railing.

12. The ship was bound for England.

13. People waved to the passengers.

14. A few people walked down the gangplank.

15. The ship would soon be sailing into the Atlantic Ocean.

Prepositional Phrases Used as Adjectives

A prepositional phrase that modifies a noun or a pronoun is an **adjective phrase**.
Examples:

    The killer whale is a species *of porpoise*. (tells what kind of species)

    That whale *with the unusual markings* is our favorite. (tells which whale)

    A pod *of twenty whales* was sighted recently. (tells how many in the pod)

DIRECTIONS → **Underline the adjective phrase or phrases in each sentence. Then write the word that the adjective phrase modifies.**

1. Sheets of ice cover Antarctica.

    _____

2. The land below the ice is always frozen.

    _____

3. Explorers with dog sleds have crossed Antarctica.

    _____

4. An admiral from the United States explored Antarctica.

    _____

5. A camp on Ross Ice Shelf was where he lived.

    _____

6. The view from the boat was spectacular.

    _____

7. The whales blew huge spouts of water.

    _____

8. The people in the boat cheered.

    _____

9. Blue whales are the largest mammals in the world.

    _____

10. The trainer of the porpoises waved her hand.

    _____

11. Many people in the crowd laughed.

    _____

12. The beginning of each show was the same.

    _____

13. The porpoises' leaps into the air were unbelievable.

    _____

14. A large pail held rewards for the performers.

    _____

15. More than two percent of Earth's surface is frozen.

    _____

16. Rivers and lakes contain one percent of that water.

    _____

17. The oceans contain the rest of the water.

    _____

18. The Pacific is the largest ocean on Earth.

    _____

Prepositional Phrases Used as Adverbs

A prepositional phrase that modifies a verb, an adjective, or an adverb is an **adverb phrase**. An adverb phrase tells *how, when, where,* or *how often*.
Examples:

The porpoises performed *with ease.* (tells how)
Shows begin *on the hour.* (tells when)
The porpoises swim *in a large tank.* (tells where)
They are rewarded *after each trick.* (tells how often)

DIRECTIONS ▷ Underline the adverb phrase in each sentence. Then write the word modified by the adverb phrase. Label that word *verb, adjective,* or *adverb.*

1. Sam Adams supported the American Revolution with enthusiasm.

    _____

2. He spoke against the English king.

    _____

3. Sam would not ride a horse, so he traveled on foot.

    _____

4. He walked far from his home, giving speeches.

    _____

5. This revolutionary was enthusiastic about freedom.

    _____

6. Whales are the largest mammals that live on Earth.

    _____

7. Whales swim in the ocean.

    _____

8. Whales behave with great intelligence.

    _____

9. A whale must breathe air through its lungs.

    _____

10. Whales can dive for long periods.

    _____

11. Oceanographers work beneath the ocean's surface.

    _____

12. They descend in small diving ships.

    _____

13. Water pressure would crush some ships in a moment.

    _____

14. These vessels are designed for quick maneuvers.

    _____

15. Some of these ships carry scientists to the ocean floor.

    _____

Choosing the Correct Preposition

Use *in* to mean "already inside." Use *into* to tell about movement from the outside to the inside.

Examples:

The groceries are *in* the house.

He took the groceries *into* the house.

Use *between* for two and *among* for three or more.

Examples:

We divided the money *between* Ruthie and Daniel.

We divided the money *among* Ruthie, Daniel, and Luther.

Use *different from* to tell about differences.

Example:

The temperatures this summer are very *different from* the temperatures of last summer.

Do not use *of* in place of *have* when you write.

Example:

CORRECT: Joy *could have* become a teacher.

INCORRECT: Joy *could of* become a teacher.

DIRECTIONS ▷ **Write the preposition in parentheses that correctly completes each sentence.**

1. Joe took a bus from the city _____ the desert.
　　　　　　　　　　　　　　　　(in, into)

2. The ride back to the city was _____ the ride to the desert.
　　　　　　　　　　　　　(different from, different than)

3. The bus broke down _____ the desert and the city.
　　　　　　　　　　　　　　(between, among)

4. The driver of a car going _____ town called for help.
　　　　　　　　　　　　　　　　(in, into)

5. The passengers wandered _____ the many desert plants while the bus was
　　　　　　　　　　　　　　(between, among)

being repaired.

6. Joe had several juice drinks _____ his pack.
　　　　　　　　　　　　　　　　(in, into)

7. He _____ kept them all for himself.
　　　　(could of, could have)

8. Instead, he divided them _____ the thirsty passengers.
　　　　　　　　　　　　　　(between, among)

9. He and another passenger had brought ten drinks _____ them.
　　　　　　　　　　　　　　　　(between, among)

Recognizing Sentences

A **sentence** expresses a complete thought.
Examples:

My father travels around the country.   The airplane has landed.

DIRECTIONS > For each group of words, write *sentence* or *not a sentence*.

1. "The Fun They Had" is a story.

   _____

2. Written by Isaac Asimov.

   _____

3. It is about two students.

   _____

4. Living in the year 2155.

   _____

5. Their teachers are machines in their homes.

   _____

6. A complicated computer.

   _____

7. Ana has been telling Hakim an amazing story.

   _____

8. It is *Fantastic Voyage*, a movie.

   _____

9. To save a dying man.

   _____

10. Scientists are shrunk to microscopic sizes.

   _____

11. A tiny submarine.

   _____

12. Into a world of unimagined complexity and beauty.

   _____

13. Dangers await these brave voyagers.

   _____

14. Through the valves of a beating heart.

   _____

DIRECTIONS > Write words to complete each sentence.

15. _____ study together.

16. Human teachers _____.

17. Today's students _____.

18. _____ would rather learn from machines.

19. _____ enjoys attending school with other students.

Four Kinds of Sentences

A **declarative sentence** makes a statement. Use a period at the end of a declarative sentence.

Example:

> Janelle is painting a picture of an imaginary place.

An **interrogative sentence** asks a question. Use a question mark at the end of an interrogative sentence.

Example:

> Who could ever create a more imaginative scene?

An **imperative sentence** gives a command or makes a request. Use a period at the end of an imperative sentence.

Example:

> Think about all the uses for artwork.

An **exclamatory sentence** expresses strong feeling. Use an exclamation point at the end of an exclamatory sentence.

Example:

> Who could ever create a more imaginative scene!

DIRECTIONS For each sentence, write *declarative, interrogative, imperative,* or *exclamatory*. Put the correct punctuation mark at the end of the sentence.

1. Look at the apes

_____

2. How clever they are

_____

3. They seem almost human

_____

4. Do you notice anything about the biggest ape

_____

5. That ape looks familiar

_____

6. Doesn't it remind you of someone

_____

7. Akiko has challenged me to a contest

_____

8. Which one of us can create the most imaginative painting

_____

DIRECTIONS Change each sentence into the kind of sentence identified in parentheses.

9. You should watch that ape. (imperative)

_____

10. It is copying my movements. (interrogative)

_____

Subjects and Predicates

Include a **subject** and a **predicate** in every sentence.
In the subject, tell whom or what the sentence is about.
Example:
> *One person* described her experience.

In the predicate, tell something about the subject.
Example:
> One person *described her experience.*

DIRECTIONS ▶ **In each sentence, underline the subject once and the predicate twice.**

1. Amelia Bloomer did not invent bloomers.
2. Bloomers were the first slacks for women.
3. These pants were very loose and comfortable.
4. Elizabeth Smith Miller became tired of long skirts and petticoats.
5. She first wore the pants in public.
6. The new outfit was described in Amelia Bloomer's newspaper.
7. People began to call the pants "bloomers."
8. Most people were shocked to see women in pants.
9. The circus began with a parade.
10. Every performer wore a glittery costume.
11. Lillie had been to the circus twice.
12. The acrobats flew through the air.
13. Our gym teacher has taught us to tumble.
14. The children bought refreshments.
15. The audience saw the animals perform.
16. Her aunt took her to the circus.
17. The work is dangerous.
18. Paolo tore his new red shirt.
19. The clowns threw candy into the crowd.
20. The family sat close to the top.

DIRECTIONS ▶ **Think of a subject or a predicate to complete each sentence. Write *subject* or *predicate* to show what to add. Then write the sentence. Remember to begin each sentence with a capital letter and end it with a punctuation mark that shows what kind of sentence it is.**

21. are awkward to wear for running _____

_____

22. different types of pants _____

_____

Complete and Simple Subjects

The **complete subject** is all the words in the subject.
Example:

> *My two older brothers* stared at me silently.

The **simple subject** is the main word or words in the subject.
Example:

> My two older *brothers* stared at me silently.

Sometimes the complete subject and the simple subject are the same.
Example:

> *Xavier* stared at me silently.

DIRECTIONS Write the complete subject of each sentence. Underline the simple subject.

1. My best friend is afraid of snakes. _____

2. Some snakes are poisonous. _____

3. Glands in the snake's head produced the venom. _____

4. Special fangs inject the poison into the victim. _____

5. The deadly venom can kill a large man. _____

6. My brothers are acting suspiciously. _____

7. Jaime took a letter out of the mailbox yesterday. _____

8. The contents of that letter mystify me. _____

9. Two classmates of mine whispered behind my back. _____

10. This secret is fun for everyone except me. _____

11. Several members of the crew were sewing costumes. _____

12. Angelina was working in the costume room. _____

13. Many costumes were still unfinished. _____

14. Other outfits needed alterations. _____

15. Four students joined the costume crew. _____

DIRECTIONS Write a complete subject for each sentence. Underline the simple subject.

16. _____ is feared by desert travelers.

17. _____ watches for poisonous snakes.

18. _____ will avoid people if possible.

Complete and Simple Predicates

The **complete predicate** is all the words in the predicate.
Example:

Everyone in my house *is keeping a secret.*

The **simple predicate** is the main word or words in the predicate.
Example:

Everyone in my house *is keeping* a secret.

Sometimes the complete predicate and the simple predicate are the same.
Example:

Everyone *smiles.*

DIRECTIONS ▷ Write the complete predicate of each sentence. Underline the simple predicate.

1. Jeff carried his board toward the water. _____

2. He paddled out toward the large breakers. _____

3. A huge wave crashed over his head. _____

4. The surf tossed the board into the air. _____

5. Grandma López says nothing to me. _____

6. The secret was revealed on Saturday afternoon. _____

7. My relatives from near and far arrived on my birthday. _____

8. Even Aunt María came. _____

9. I had a wonderful, fantastic party. _____

10. The pink eraser bounced onto the floor. _____

11. Miles stared at the eraser for five minutes. _____

12. Every rubbery side stretched. _____

13. The enormous eraser bumped into the teacher's desk. _____

14. The entire class watched the eraser with amazement. _____

15. Mrs. Reyna quickly picked it up. _____

Finding Subjects of Sentences

To find the simple subject of an interrogative sentence, first make it declarative. Then, ask whom or what it is about.
Example:
    Did *Sandra Cisneros* write that book?
Remember that the simple subject of an imperative sentence is usually not stated but is understood to be *you*.
Example:
    (*You*) Read that book.
In a declarative sentence that begins with *here* or *there*, look for the simple subject after the predicate.
Example:
    There are many *books* to read.

DIRECTIONS ➤ Write the simple subject of each sentence. Then write *declarative*, *interrogative*, *imperative*, or *exclamatory* to tell what kind of sentence it is.

1. Are the new neighbors home today?

   _____

   _____

2. There was a woman in the house an hour ago.

   _____

   _____

3. Where did she go?

   _____

   _____

4. Have you met them?

   _____

   _____

5. Here is a newspaper article about them.

   _____

   _____

6. Are there any children in the family?

   _____

   _____

7. There was a boy in the yard.

   _____

   _____

8. There is a puppy in the yard now.

   _____

   _____

9. How cute that puppy is!

   _____

   _____

10. Come to me.

   _____

   _____

Compound Subjects

Two or more simple subjects with the same predicate are called a **compound subject**.
The simple subjects in a compound subject are usually joined by *and* or *or*.
Example:

Jon and Stacy congratulated the actress.

To save words, combine sentences with similar predicates into one sentence with a compound subject.
Example:

The *members* of the cast were nervous. The *director* was nervous.
The *members* of the cast and the *director* were nervous.

DIRECTIONS ➤ **Write the complete subject of each sentence. Then, underline each simple subject, and circle the connecting word.**

1. A tornado or a hurricane is very dangerous.

   _____

2. Lightning and the force of wind can destroy a town.

   _____

3. A person, a large animal, or an automobile may be hurled in the air.

   _____

4. My aunt, my uncle, and my younger cousin saw a tornado.

   _____

5. Dark clouds and powerful winds warned them of the approaching storm.

   _____

6. My aunt and uncle knew what to do.

   _____

7. The family, the cat, and the dog went to the cellar.

   _____

8. Their house and garage were left standing.

   _____

9. The school and the house across the street were badly damaged.

   _____

Compound Predicates

Two or more predicates with the same subject are called **compound predicates**.
The simple predicates in a compound predicate are usually joined by *and* or *or*.
Example:
    We *will find* the card catalog or *will ask* the librarian for help.

◎◎◎◎◎◎◎◎◎◎◎◎◎◎◎◎◎◎◎◎◎◎◎◎◎◎◎◎◎◎◎◎◎◎◎◎◎◎

DIRECTIONS ▷ **Write the complete predicate of each sentence. Then, underline each simple predicate, and circle the connecting word.**

1. The traffic light flashed for a few minutes and then turned red.

    _____

2. The cars slowed and finally stopped.

    _____

3. Candace reached over and adjusted the radio.

    _____

4. The announcer reported on traffic conditions and advised drivers.

    _____

5. Several drivers heard the report and chose a different route.

    _____

6. The three of us whispered, pointed, and made notes.

    _____

7. Twelve astronauts walked or drove across the dusty moonscape during the three and a half years
    of moon landings.

    _____

8. They took soil samples, measured temperatures, and tested the lunar gravity.

    _____

9. Back in orbit, the astronauts released the lunar module and measured the vibrations from its impact.

    _____

10. *Apollo 17*'s return to Earth brought the mission to a close and marked the end of manned
    moon landings.

    _____

Compound Sentences

Use a **simple sentence** to express one complete thought.
Example:
> Objects from space fall into the atmosphere.

Combine two or more simple sentences to make a **compound sentence**. The simple sentences can by joined by a comma and connecting words such as *and, or,* or *but,* or by a semicolon.
Example:
> A crater can be formed by a bomb, or it can be formed by a meteorite.

DIRECTIONS For each sentence write *compound subject, compound predicate,* or *compound sentence.*

1. Jesse and Carroll watched a game show on television.

   _____

2. It was boring, and Carroll felt restless.

   _____

3. Carroll likes animals and prefers shows about wildlife.

   _____

4. Carroll called Jim, and he invited her over.

   _____

5. At Jim's house, Carroll and Jim enjoyed a film about dolphins.

   _____

6. Some meteors grow hot and burn up.

   _____

7. Metal or stone sometimes reaches the ground.

   _____

8. Friction makes meteors incredibly hot, and they burn up miles above Earth's surface.

   _____

9. Some large meteors do not burn up completely; they are called meteorites.

   _____

10. Have you or Becky seen the Meteor Crater in Arizona?

    _____

11. A meteorite exploded over Siberia and created more than 200 craters.

    _____

12. A meteorite crashed there perhaps 50,000 years ago, or it may have fallen earlier.

    _____

13. The Americans and the Russians have sent rockets into space.

    _____

14. My friends came, but they left early.

    _____

15. Robin or Kelly is on the telephone.

    _____

16. Elena chose the program Monday night; Ryan chose it Tuesday.

    _____

Conjunctions

Use a **conjunction** to join words or groups of words. A conjunction can be *and, or,* or *but.*
Example:
    Palak *or* Chris has a cell phone.
A conjunction can be used to combine sentences.
Example:
    Janet lives in Austin, *and* Elizabeth lives in New Braunfels.

DIRECTIONS ➤ Circle the conjunction in each sentence. Then underline the words or groups of words it joins.

1. Florence Nightingale was the daughter of an English squire, but she was born in Florence, Italy.

2. She was raised and educated in Derbyshire, England.

3. Florence did not want to be idle or useless.

4. Nursing was not considered a proper occupation for ladies, but Florence was determined to be a nurse.

5. Florence went to Germany and studied nursing.

6. Llamas are quite gentle, and people often make pets of them.

7. Llamas climb easily over rocky terrain and make good pack animals in the mountains.

8. A llama is not carnivorous and prefers grass and leaves as food.

9. Sandra and Larry have a pet llama.

10. Llamas emit a humming sound, and you can hear it.

11. The llama lacks speech organs and is mute.

12. Sally talked to one expert, and he told her something interesting.

13. An angry llama will pull its ears back and spit.

14. Grasses and leaves are a llama's main source of food.

15. Llamas enjoy human company and are quite affectionate.

DIRECTIONS ➤ Rewrite each pair of sentences as one sentence. Use the conjunction in parentheses to join words or groups of words.

16. Florence returned to London. She became the supervisor of a hospital. (and)

_____

17. England entered the war. Florence joined the War Office as a nurse. (and)

_____

Interjections

An **interjection** is a word or a group of words that expresses strong feeling. You can separate an interjection from the rest of a sentence with either an exclamation point or a comma, depending on the strength of the feeling.

Examples:

    Whew!   That was close!   Oh, no!   That is the wrong answer!

DIRECTIONS ▸ Write the interjection from each sentence. Label each one *strong* or *mild*.

1. Say, isn't Mary pitching today? _____

2. Hooray! We get to bat first. _____

3. Well, the team is in good shape. _____

4. Wow! Look at that pitch! _____

5. Hey! That should have been a strike! _____

DIRECTIONS ▸ Add an interjection to each sentence. Write the new sentence. Add punctuation marks where they are needed.

6. That's the way to pitch.

    _____

7. She missed that one.

    _____

8. She'll hit it next time.

    _____

9. What a hit she made!

    _____

10. Look at her go!

    _____

DIRECTIONS ▸ Write sentences using the following interjections: *yikes, ugh, ssh,* and *bravo.*

_____

_____

_____

_____

Avoiding Sentence Fragments and Run-on Sentences

Avoid using a **sentence fragment**, which does not express a complete thought.
Example:
>   Tells an interesting story.

Avoid using a **run-on sentence**, which strings together two or more sentences without clearly separating them.
Example:
>   This picture is his it is not yours.

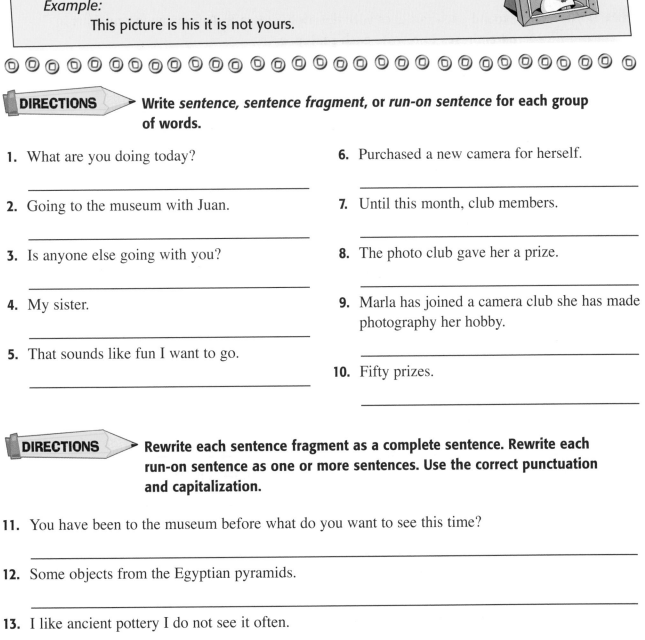

◎◎◎◎◎◎◎◎◎◎◎◎◎◎◎◎◎◎◎◎◎◎◎◎◎◎◎◎◎◎◎◎◎

DIRECTIONS ➤ Write *sentence, sentence fragment,* or *run-on sentence* for each group of words.

1. What are you doing today?

   _____

2. Going to the museum with Juan.

   _____

3. Is anyone else going with you?

   _____

4. My sister.

   _____

5. That sounds like fun I want to go.

   _____

6. Purchased a new camera for herself.

   _____

7. Until this month, club members.

   _____

8. The photo club gave her a prize.

   _____

9. Marla has joined a camera club she has made photography her hobby.

   _____

10. Fifty prizes.

    _____

DIRECTIONS ➤ Rewrite each sentence fragment as a complete sentence. Rewrite each run-on sentence as one or more sentences. Use the correct punctuation and capitalization.

11. You have been to the museum before what do you want to see this time?

   _____

12. Some objects from the Egyptian pyramids.

   _____

13. I like ancient pottery I do not see it often.

   _____

Expanding Sentences

Sentences can be **expanded** by adding details to make them clearer and more interesting.
Example:
> The waitress smiled.
> The waitress in the red dress smiled happily to the customers.

DIRECTIONS → Expand each sentence with descriptive details. Follow the instructions in parentheses to rewrite each sentence.

1. A dog huddled in the shelter of the tunnel. (Add details about the subject.)

    _____

2. It shivered in the wind. (Add descriptive details about an item in the complete predicate.)

    _____

3. Finally, it left the shelter of the tunnel. (Add another predicate.)

    _____

4. Its shadow trailed behind it. (Add descriptive details about the subject.)

    _____

5. The dog trotted down the street. (Add another subject.)

    _____

6. The dog broke through the sheet of ice on the puddle. (Add descriptive details about an item in the complete predicate and add a second predicate.)

    _____

    _____

7. The curtain slowly opens. (Add details about the subject.)

    _____

8. I remember the drive. (Add descriptive details about an item in the complete predicate.)

    _____

9. We drove from Tucson to the Grand Canyon. (Add another predicate.)

    _____

10. The girl blew out the candles. (Add descriptive details about an item in the complete predicate and add a second predicate.)

    _____

    _____

Correcting Sentence Fragments and Run-on Sentences

Good writers correct sentence fragments and run-on sentences.
Example:
INCORRECT: The boys were hungry we made hot dogs.
CORRECT: The boys were hungry, so we made hot dogs.

DIRECTIONS ▶ **Rewrite the following paragraphs from a business letter. Correct any sentence fragments or run-on sentences.**

I should begin by telling you how long I have been a customer of Ronnie's. For five years. I have always been satisfied with your merchandise and your service.

I am happy to have an opportunity to tell you how much I have enjoyed shopping at Ronnie's. However, my letter has a different purpose. To ask you to carry my favorite line of sporting goods. Sporty's. I have begun shopping elsewhere for sporting goods. I would rather be shopping at Ronnie's it is my favorite store. Besides, your other customers would enjoy Sporty's top-quality goods. Available at Ronnie's low prices.

Please consider my suggestion let me know what you decide.

Phrases and Clauses

A **phrase** is a group of words that work together. A phrase does not have both a subject and a predicate.
Example:
    from the kitchen window
A **clause** is a group of words that has a subject and a predicate. Some clauses can stand alone as sentences; others cannot.
Example:
    Everyone should know about medical emergencies.

DIRECTIONS ▸ Write *phrase* or *clause* to identify each group of words.

1. we enjoy living in this town _____

2. near friendly, helpful neighbors _____

3. from the nearest ocean _____

4. since they moved to Ohio _____

5. between a rushing stream and a grassy slope _____

6. we built a cabin _____

7. from fragrant pine logs _____

8. in the huge stone fireplace _____

9. you can read first-aid manuals _____

10. although my aunt does not have a medical degree _____

11. while Eric played outside _____

12. in Joseph's construction site _____

13. she saved someone's life _____

DIRECTIONS ▸ Complete each sentence. Add the kind of word group named in parentheses.

14. When I grow up, _____.
                              (clause)

15. I want to live _____.
                              (phrase)

16. _____, who is my best friend.
                  (clause)

17. After he examined Leah, the doctor said, "You have been bitten _____."
                                                                        (phrase)

Independent and Dependent Clauses

An **independent clause** expresses a complete thought and can stand alone as a simple sentence.

Examples:

> *Some pollution affects our homes and schools.*
> If their neighbors cooperate, *young people and adults can clean up their neighborhoods.*

A **dependent clause** contains a subject and a predicate, but it does not express a complete thought and it cannot stand alone.

Example:

> People became more sensitive to pollution problems *after they learned about toxic waste.*

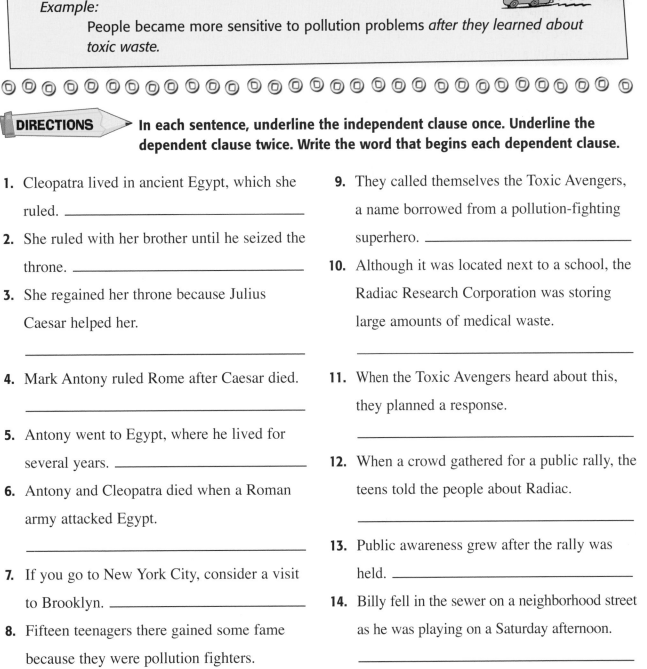

DIRECTIONS ➤ **In each sentence, underline the independent clause once. Underline the dependent clause twice. Write the word that begins each dependent clause.**

1. Cleopatra lived in ancient Egypt, which she ruled. _____

2. She ruled with her brother until he seized the throne. _____

3. She regained her throne because Julius Caesar helped her.

   _____

4. Mark Antony ruled Rome after Caesar died.

   _____

5. Antony went to Egypt, where he lived for several years. _____

6. Antony and Cleopatra died when a Roman army attacked Egypt.

   _____

7. If you go to New York City, consider a visit to Brooklyn. _____

8. Fifteen teenagers there gained some fame because they were pollution fighters.

   _____

9. They called themselves the Toxic Avengers, a name borrowed from a pollution-fighting superhero. _____

10. Although it was located next to a school, the Radiac Research Corporation was storing large amounts of medical waste.

    _____

11. When the Toxic Avengers heard about this, they planned a response.

    _____

12. When a crowd gathered for a public rally, the teens told the people about Radiac.

    _____

13. Public awareness grew after the rally was held. _____

14. Billy fell in the sewer on a neighborhood street as he was playing on a Saturday afternoon.

    _____

Compound and Complex Sentences

A **compound sentence** consists of two or more independent clauses.
Example:
> Fires are dangerous, and they cause great damage.

A **complex sentence** consists of an independent clause and at least one dependent clause. Dependent clauses often tell *why, when, where, what,* or *which one.*
A dependent clause that begins a sentence is usually followed by a comma.
Example:
> *Because someone had been careless with matches*, a fire started at the Johnsons' home. (tells *why*)

A dependent clause that comes at the end of the sentence is usually not preceded by a comma.
Example:
> Smoke filled the house *as firefighters arrived*. (tells *when*)

When a dependent clause comes in the middle of a sentence, it is usually set off by commas.
Example:
> The fire, *which we saw spreading rapidly*, shot sparks into the sky.
> (tells *which one*)

DIRECTIONS ▸ Write *compound* or *complex* to identify each sentence.

1. Aristotle lived in ancient Greece, and he became a great philosopher.

   _____

2. Since philosophers enjoy thinking about life, they also enjoy discussing it with others.

   _____

3. Because Plato was a famous philosopher, Aristotle attended his school.

   _____

4. Aristotle became famous himself, and many people studied his work.

   _____

5. Aristotle taught Alexander the Great before Alexander became king of Macedonia.

   _____

6. Aristotle started his own school when he received money from Alexander.

   _____

7. *Tsunami* is a Japanese word for tidal wave, but these waves occur around the world.

   _____

8. Some tidal waves begin after an earthquake occurs.

   _____

9. The worst recorded earthquake in history took place in 1201, and about one million people died.

   _____

10. Earthquakes are measured using a scale that was devised by Charles Richter and Beno Gutenberg.

    _____

Compound and Complex Sentences

Capitalization and End Punctuation

Begin every written sentence with a capital letter.
Example:
> Let's go to the zoo.

End a declarative sentence with a period.
Example:
> I can go, too.

End an interrogative sentence with a question mark.
Example:
> Can Mark go with us?

End an exclamatory sentence with an exclamation point.
Example:
> Of course you can go!

DIRECTIONS ➤ **Rewrite each sentence. Add a capital letter and the correct end punctuation.**

1. have you ever lost your voice

   _____

2. what a strange feeling that is

   _____

3. you try to talk, but you can only squeak

   _____

4. no one can understand you

   _____

5. the climbers left their base camp at six in the morning

   _____

6. mr. Enami is a train engineer

   _____

7. miles found his math problems to be very challenging

   _____

8. does the community softball league meet every Friday

   _____

9. pedro and I go to the museum in California

   _____

10. he is such a conscientious student

    _____

Commas and Semicolons

Use commas to separate words or phrases in a series.
Example:
> I studied for the test on *Monday, Tuesday*, and *Wednesday*.

Use commas to set off mild interjections.
Example:
> *Wow*, I did really well on the test!

Use commas and conjunctions, or use semicolons, to separate the clauses in compound sentences.
Examples:
> The book is entertaining, and interested people should read it.
> The book is entertaining; interested people should read it.

Use a comma after a dependent clause that begins a complex sentence.
Example:
> After I studied for the test, I passed it.

DIRECTIONS ➤ Add commas or semicolons where they are needed in each sentence.

1. As her plane touched down on the small runway Amanda felt excited.

2. Lucia made a dollhouse out of construction paper cardboard and fabric.

3. Her luggage was soon unloaded sorted and returned to her.

4. If you want to see her call her on the telephone.

5. Jon helped Amanda carry her gear and they walked out to the truck.

6. Ms. Rivera teaches Greek Latin and classical literature.

7. Hey did you decide to write a letter to the editor of the paper?

8. Although you may not agree I think people should join together to fight for a cause.

9. Do Noah Carrie and Katy still volunteer?

10. Many people were traveling to Dallas Phoenix and Los Angeles.

11. The weather is getting worse we should cancel the outdoor concert.

12. The pilot copilot and navigator flew us through the storm safely.

13. Oh I thought I'd surprise you!

14. Paula North is our team captain Shu Lee is her assistant.

15. Although the director thought the film was great the audiences walked out.

16. Even though the wind is low the boy tries to fly a kite.

Capitalization of Proper Nouns, Proper Adjectives, and *I*

Capitalize proper nouns and proper adjectives.
Examples:
> November, Chicago, Republican, American

Capitalize the pronoun *I*.
Examples:
> I am here.   Lynn and I are here.

DIRECTIONS > **Rewrite each item correctly.**

1. beth ann drake _____

2. president lincoln _____

3. central Bookstore _____

4. waco, texas _____

5. logan, utah _____

6. italian marble _____

7. me, myself, and i _____

8. english accent _____

9. union army _____

10. american citizen _____

11. adams middle school _____

12. *beauty and the beast* _____

13. latin club _____

14. amelia earhart boulevard _____

15. declaration of independence _____

16. yellowstone national park _____

17. mexican pottery _____

18. new year's day _____

Abbreviations

Use a period after most **abbreviations**.
Examples:
> adj. (adjective)　　　Blvd. (Boulevard)

Capitalize abbreviations that stand for proper nouns.
Examples:
> Sat. (Saturday)　　　Oct. (October)

Do not use periods when writing postal abbreviations of the fifty states or the abbreviations of some large organizations.
Examples:
> NH (New Hampshire)　　NATO (North Atlantic Treaty Organization)

Do not use periods for units of measure unless the abbreviation forms a word. (in., gal.)
Examples:
> cm (centimeter)　　　km (kilometer)

DIRECTIONS Write a correct abbreviation of each term. Use a dictionary, if necessary.

1. pound _____
2. ounce _____
3. foot _____
4. yard _____
5. Maine _____
6. milligram _____
7. liter _____
8. cubic centimeter _____
9. United States Postal Service _____
10. National Basketball Association _____

11. Rodeo Drive _____
12. Old Post Road _____
13. Fifth Avenue _____
14. National Collegiate Athletic Association _____
15. medical doctor _____
16. miles per hour _____
17. revolutions per minute _____
18. Fahrenheit _____
19. Celsius _____

DIRECTIONS Rewrite each group of words, using abbreviations. Use initials for middle names.

20. Best Carpet Cleaners, Incorporated _____
21. The Farley Farragut Company _____
22. Doctor Thomas Francis Gorman _____

More Abbreviations

Use an abbreviation, or shortened form of a word, to save space when you write lists and addresses or fill out forms.

To write an initial, use the first letter of a name followed by a period.

◎◎◎◎◎◎◎◎◎◎◎◎◎◎◎◎◎◎◎◎◎◎◎◎◎◎◎◎◎◎◎◎◎◎

DIRECTIONS Imagine that you are filling out an application for a job. Write the information in the chart below. Capitalize and punctuate each abbreviation and initial correctly.

JOE BOB'S RESTAURANT

Name: _____

Street address: _____

Birth date: _____

Date of application: _____

DIRECTIONS Use abbreviations whenever possible to complete the form with the following information: 120 Grant Avenue; The Parker School; Helena Moreno Ramírez; September 4, 2005; Ponca City, Oklahoma.

STUDENT INFORMATION CARD

School: _____

Address: _____

_____

Principal: _____

First Day of School: _____

◎◎◎◎◎◎◎◎◎◎◎◎◎◎◎◎◎◎◎◎◎◎◎◎◎◎◎◎◎◎◎◎◎

Titles

Capitalize the first word, the last word, and all the important words in a title. Underline the titles of books, plays, magazines, newspapers, television shows, and movies. If you are using a computer, replace underlining with italics.
Examples:

      60 Minutes, The Secret Garden, Los Angeles Times, Pinocchio

Place quotation marks around the titles of short works, such as poems, short stories, chapters, articles, and songs.
Examples:

      "Little Miss Muffet," "America the Beautiful"

DIRECTIONS ➤ Circle the words in each title that should be capitalized.

1. around the world in eighty days

2. the pirates of penzance

3. profiles in courage

4. stalking the wild asparagus

5. the cat ate my gymsuit

6. "shake, rattle, and roll"

7. "twist and shout"

8. "me and my shadow"

9. the red balloon

10. the wizard of oz

DIRECTIONS ➤ Write the title in each sentence correctly.

11. The movie stand by me is one of my favorites.

    _____

12. Did you know it is based on a short story called the body?

    _____

13. The story was written by Stephen King, who also wrote the novels cujo, christine, and carrie.

    _____

14. The title of the movie comes from one of the best songs in it, stand by me.

    _____

15. Where is last week's issue of time?

    _____

16. Have you read John Steinbeck's book travels with charley?

    _____

17. I just found that article, welcome to Pittsburgh.

    _____

18. My family enjoys watching Monday night football.

    _____

19. Did you see that movie about Dian Fossey called gorillas in the mist?

    _____

Direct Quotations and Dialogue

Use quotation marks before and after a **direct quotation**.
Example:
  "The truth is powerful and will prevail," said Sojourner Truth.
If a quotation is interrupted by other words, place quotation marks around the quoted words only.
Example:
  "Give me liberty," Patrick Henry cried, "or give me death!"
Place a comma or a period inside closing quotation marks.
Example:
  "I have read those words before," said Ben.
Place a question mark or an exclamation point inside closing quotation marks if the quotation itself is a question or an exclamation.
Example:
  "Haven't you ever heard of Sojourner Truth or Patrick Henry?" asked Marcia.

DIRECTIONS ▸ Rewrite each sentence using correct punctuation and capitalization.

1. Leon dragged the huge crate through and shouted I'm home, Mom!

   _____

2. She isn't back yet Leon's brother told him.

   _____

3. Oh, Leon said his brother, staring at the box what is that?

   _____

4. Queen Elizabeth I ruled a great empire, Marcia said.

   _____

5. She told her critics, I have the heart and stomach of a king.

   _____

6. Who else had a great impact on a country? asked Terri.

   _____

7. Well, Ben remarked, Mohandas Gandhi inspired a nonviolent revolution in India.

   _____

8. Gandhi inspired Martin Luther King! Terri added.

   _____

9. New York has a new program, Nancy said, for student ticket buyers.

   _____

Appositives

An **appositive** is a noun or a noun phrase that identifies or renames the word or words that precede it. Use commas to set off an appositive from the rest of the sentence.
Examples:

Our steward, *James Moreno*, speaks three languages.
His home is in Rome, *the capital of Italy*.

DIRECTIONS ▶ Rewrite each sentence correctly. Use commas where they are needed. Then underline the appositive. Circle the noun or pronoun it tells about.

1. The company High Flyers forgot to include instructions.

   _____

2. The Eagle our only car would not start.

   _____

3. Our neighbor Jim Delgado came to help.

   _____

4. Even Jim a good mechanic could not start it.

   _____

5. The starter an electric motor was not working.

   _____

6. The pilot Captain Songrossi said to fasten our seat belts.

   _____

7. A prairie a kind of grassland is home to many kinds of plants and animals.

   _____

8. Our teacher Ms. Pesek does not agree.

   _____

9. Our store Video Visions has many unusual movies.

   _____

10. The film an exciting dinosaur story is filed with other adventure films.

   _____

DIRECTIONS ▶ Rewrite the sentences, using appositives to add information.

11. Our school is open all year. _____

12. I would like to see my favorite film again.

   _____

Contractions

Form **contractions** by putting two words together and replacing one or more letters with an apostrophe.
Examples:
    is not = isn't, it is = it's, you will = you'll

DIRECTIONS ➤ Write the contraction in each sentence and the words from which it was formed.

1. I'd like to learn to ski. _____

2. I've asked Susan to teach me. _____

3. I know she's an excellent skier. _____

4. She says it isn't difficult. _____

5. We've asked Tom and Jack to come with us. _____

6. They've been skiing for years. _____

7. I'm working at a grocery store after school. _____

8. We aren't going to be able to sleep tonight. _____

9. Xavier didn't play football today. _____

10. They'd be here if they could. _____

11. Tiffany wasn't feeling well today. _____

12. Eloisa and Pete haven't been home all weekend. _____

13. You've signed up to take a weaving class. _____

14. Lina can't close the door. _____

15. Doesn't the mural look great? _____

DIRECTIONS ➤ Write a sentence using the contraction for each pair of words.

16. should not _____

17. will not _____

18. he would _____

19. let us _____

20. you are _____

Synonyms and Antonyms

> **Synonyms** are two or more words that have the same or similar meanings.
> *Examples:*
>   bush—shrub, dogs—hounds, shoved—pushed
> **Antonyms** are words that have opposite meanings.
> *Examples:*
>   old—new, young—old, awake—asleep

DIRECTIONS ➤ **Read the paragraphs. Write a synonym or an antonym for the underlined word in the space provided.**

Annette had been <u>ill (1)</u> for a week. The day she returned, class had already <u>begun (2)</u>. She was <u>late (3)</u> because she had to stop at the office on her way to the classroom.

Annette had missed an <u>examination (4)</u>. Mr. Castellanos sent her to a desk in the <u>rear (5)</u> of the room to make it up. There was <u>nobody (6)</u> at the desk to the right of Annette's, but Roland was sitting in the desk to the <u>right (7)</u>.

The teacher told the students to be <u>quiet (8)</u> until Annette had finished the examination. When the class <u>left (9)</u> for recess, Annette stayed behind to <u>finish (10)</u> the examination. The examination was not <u>difficult (11)</u>. Annette was sure that all her answers were <u>correct (12)</u>.

1. (synonym) _____

2. (synonym) _____

3. (antonym) _____

4. (synonym) _____

5. (synonym) _____

6. (synonym) _____

7. (antonym) _____

8. (antonym) _____

9. (antonym) _____

10. (antonym) _____

11. (antonym) _____

12. (synonym) _____

DIRECTIONS ➤ **Complete the chart by writing one synonym and one antonym for each word in the first column.**

Word	Synonym	Antonym
13. wild	_____	_____
14. bolder	_____	_____
15. thick	_____	_____
16. fortunate	_____	_____
17. mend	_____	_____
18. gather	_____	_____

Homographs and Homonyms

> **Homographs** are words that are spelled alike but have different meanings.
> *Examples:*
> The karate students *bow* to one another.
> I made a red *bow* to put on top of the wrapped gift.

◎◎◎◎◎◎◎◎◎◎◎◎◎◎◎◎◎◎◎◎◎◎◎◎◎◎◎◎◎◎◎◎◎◎

> **DIRECTIONS** For each item, circle the correct meaning of the underlined word.

1. When Annemarie heard a <u>light</u> tapping at the door after curfew, she knew something was wrong.

   brightness   gentle

2. As her parents explained that the Rosens had gone into hiding, Annemarie could see that their faces were <u>drawn</u> with worry.

   sketched   pulled tight

3. Kristi believed that there had been fireworks for her birthday, but the truth was the bright light had come from the burning of the Danish <u>fleet</u>.

   a group of ships   swift

4. To disguise Ellen's identity, Annemarie pulled on her friend's necklace so hard that it <u>broke</u>, and then she hid it in her hand.

   cracked into pieces   without money

> **Homonyms** are words that sound alike but have different meanings and spellings.
> *Examples:*
> write—right, flour—flower

◎◎◎◎◎◎◎◎◎◎◎◎◎◎◎◎◎◎◎◎◎◎◎◎◎◎◎◎◎◎◎◎◎◎

> **DIRECTIONS** Complete each sentence by writing the correct homonym.

5. (air, heir) Prince Chang wanted to reward Tang for the merry _____ he fiddled, and before Chang could stop himself, he let slip that he was _____ to the throne.

6. (rode, road) A group of enemy soldiers _____ their horses down the _____ to challenge Prince Chang as he traveled in disguise.

7. (throne, thrown) The prince was nearly _____ to the ground and killed, but he was saved by Lang the archer. Later, the fortunate prince took the _____ as the new king.

8. (sighed, side) Hostile soldiers gathered at the _____ of the river to attack Chang's kingdom, but they _____ with homesickness when they heard Tang play his fiddle.

◎◎◎◎◎◎◎◎◎◎◎◎◎◎◎◎◎◎◎◎◎◎◎◎◎◎◎◎◎◎◎◎ **85**

Prefixes

A **prefix** is a letter or group of letters that can be added to the beginning of a base word to change its meaning.

Example:

> *extra*, meaning "outside of, beyond" + the base word *ordinary* = *extraordinary*, meaning "beyond ordinary"

Some prefixes have one meaning, and others have more than one meaning.

Examples:

Prefix	Meaning
im	not
in	not
over	too much, over
post	after
pre	before
re	back, again
un	not

DIRECTIONS Read each sentence. Write the word formed with a prefix and underline the prefix. Then write the meaning of the word.

1. I have been inactive in the organization all year.

_____

2. I thought the audience was impolite during the speeches.

_____

3. They should not prejudge the candidates before hearing what they have to say.

_____

4. It is unusual to have this many candidates.

_____

5. I think Greg is overconfident.

_____

6. He has already ordered food for his postelection celebration.

_____

7. I hope it was inexpensive.

_____

8. Last year the committee members had to recount the ballots.

_____

Suffixes

A **suffix** is a letter or letters added to the end of a base word to change the meaning of a word.
Example:

ful, meaning "full of" + the base word *wonder* = *wonderful*, meaning "full of wonder"

DIRECTIONS Read each sentence. Write the word formed with a suffix. After each word, write the suffix.

1. "You look thoughtful," said Richard.

   _____

2. "I was just looking at those grayish clouds," replied Louise.

   _____

3. "I think it may be a rainy night."

   _____

4. "Yes," agreed Richard. "The cows sound restless."

   _____

5. "Do you think the rain will be harmful to the hay we have cut?" asked Louise.

   _____

DIRECTIONS Match the suffixes with the base words to make 18 nouns. Write the nouns on the lines.

Suffixes									
ant	ent	er	or	ist	tion	ation	ance	ence	ment

Base Words								
attend	box	celebrate	contest	compete	cycle	determine	develop	
dominate	excel	organize	perfect	prominent	revere	salute	ski	

6. _____

7. _____

8. _____

9. _____

10. _____

11. _____

12. _____

13. _____

14. _____

15. _____

16. _____

17. _____

18. _____

19. _____

20. _____

21. _____

22. _____

23. _____

Compound Words

A **compound word** is a word that is made up of two or more words. The meaning of many compound words is related to the meaning of each individual word.
Example:

> rattle + snake = rattlesnake, meaning "snake that makes a rattling sound"

Compound words may be written as one word, as hyphenated words, or as two separate words.
Examples:

> shoelace, sister-in-law, orange juice

DIRECTIONS ➤ Underline the compound word in each sentence.

1. Ron and Diane went to visit their great-uncle.

2. He lives in a three-bedroom house on the beach.

3. The beach is at the foot of a mountain range.

4. Everyone wanted to go for a walk on the beach.

5. The cuckoo clock sounded when they left.

6. They had two hours before sunset.

7. Piles of seaweed had washed up on the sand.

8. Ron noticed a jellyfish on one of the piles.

9. Diane found a starfish farther down the beach.

10. They looked out across the blue-green water.

11. Diane spotted a sea lion on a distant rock.

12. The shadows of the palm trees were growing longer.

13. They walked back, watching the fast-sinking sun.

14. They were three-fourths of the way back when the sun set.

15. The beachfront was quiet.

16. Diane was spellbound by its beauty.

17. Ron found an old inner tube.

18. They sat down to read the newspaper.

19. Jess is a jack-of-all-trades.

20. Alicia lost her earring.

DIRECTIONS ➤ Answer the following questions.

21. A *rehearsal* is "a practice for a performance." What is a *dress rehearsal*?

_____

22. *Scare* means "to frighten." What is a *scarecrow*?

_____

23. A *date* is "a particular point or period of time." What is *up-to-date*?

_____

24. A *guide* is "something serving to indicate or direct." What is a *guideword*?

_____

Denotations and Connotations: Word Overtones

> The **denotation** of a word is its exact meaning as stated in a dictionary.
> *Example:*
> The denotation of *skinny* is "very thin."
> The **connotation** of a word is an added meaning that suggests something positive or negative.
> *Examples:*
> Negative: *Skinny* suggests "too thin." *Skinny* has a negative connotation.
> Positive: *Slender* suggests "attractively thin." *Slender* has a positive connotation.

 **DIRECTIONS** Read each of these statements about Ted's Restaurant. Underline the word in parentheses that has the more positive connotation.

1. Ted's Restaurant is furnished with (old, antique) furniture.

2. The servers are all (young, immature).

3. You can sit at a table or in a (cozy, cramped) booth.

4. The service at Ted's is (slow, unhurried).

5. Ted's serves very (simple, plain) food.

6. One of the specialties is (rare, undercooked) steak.

7. (Blackened, Burned) prime rib is another.

8. Customers (sip, gulp) their cold drinks.

 **DIRECTIONS** Read each of these statements about Ted's Restaurant. Underline the word in parentheses that has the more negative connotation.

9. The beef at Ted's Restaurant is (firm, tough) and juicy.

10. The pies are (rich, greasy) with butter.

11. The crust is so (crumbly, flaky), it falls apart.

12. A (moist, soggy) cake is also available for dessert.

13. A group of (loud, enthusiastic) regulars eats at Ted's every Saturday night.

14. The steaks at Ted's are cooked over a charbroiled (flame, inferno).

Idioms

An **idiom** is an expression that has a meaning different from the usual meanings of the individual words within it.
Example:

Pull my leg means "to tease," not "to physically pull on my leg."

DIRECTIONS Read the dialogue and underline the idioms. Then rewrite the dialogue. Replace each idiom with a word or words that state the meaning of the idiom in the sentence.

"What's the matter? Has the cat got your tongue?" demanded Randy. "Tell me where we're going tonight."

"Just hold your horses," said Lester. "I told you it's a surprise. It will knock your socks off when we get there. In the meantime, get off my back."

"I can't help it," said Joe. "I've been on pins and needles all day."

"I have to keep my nose to the grindstone until I finish my chores," said Lester. "Then we can take off."

"Well, get on the ball and finish," said Randy. "I'm about to burst with curiosity."

"Lend me a hand, then," said Joe.

_____

_____

_____

_____

_____

_____

_____

_____

_____

_____

_____

_____

Subject-Verb Agreement

Use the singular form of a verb with a singular subject.
Example:
> Leo *catches* fish.

Use the plural form of a verb with a plural subject.
Example:
> Leo and I *catch* fish.

DIRECTIONS → **Write the verb in parentheses that correctly completes each sentence.**

1. Our country _____ an election for president every four years.
   (holds, hold)

2. Each party _____ a candidate.
   (selects, select)

3. Every candidate _____ his or her ideas in speeches.
   (presents, present)

4. The candidates _____ all over the country.
   (travels, travel)

5. Groups of reporters _____ the candidates.
   (follows, follow)

6. We _____ about the candidates for months.
   (hears, hear)

7. Unfortunately, some people _____ the election.
   (ignores, ignore)

8. Only voters _____ the president.
   (elects, elect)

9. The president's decisions _____ the lives of all citizens.
   (affects, affect)

10. Not every citizen _____ .
    (votes, vote)

11. Some people even _____ to register.
    (fails, fail)

12. Most candidates _____ their ideas with the voters.
    (shares, share)

13. Each voter _____ an opportunity to decide which candidate has the best ideas.
    (has, have)

14. Anna _____ her bowling ball down the lane.
    (hurls, hurl)

15. The ball _____ the target.
    (hits, hit)

Agreement of Verbs with Compound Subjects

When the parts of a compound subject are joined by *and*, use a plural verb.
Example:

Pluto and Jupiter *are* planets.

When the parts of a compound subject are joined by *or* or *nor*, use the verb form that agrees with the subject closest to it.
Examples:

Neither the cat nor the *puppies have* eaten yet.

Neither the puppies nor the *cat has* eaten yet.

DIRECTIONS ➤ **Write the verb in parentheses that correctly completes each sentence.**

1. Jolene and her brother _____ to read about animal defenses.
(likes, like)

2. An encyclopedia and a science book _____ good references.
(is, are)

3. Fight or flight _____ an animal's usual response to danger.
(is, are)

4. Shell and armor _____ good protection.
(provides, provide)

5. Size and strength _____ some attackers.
(discourages, discourage)

6. A snarl and a menacing look _____ others away.
(frightens, frighten)

7. An antelope or a mustang _____ an attacker.
(outruns, outrun)

8. Robins and bluebirds _____ away.
(flies, fly)

9. A lion or a tiger _____ with teeth and claws.
(fights, fight)

10 A chameleon or some fish _____ color to blend into surroundings.
(changes, change)

11. A turtle or a tortoise _____ in its shell.
(hides, hide)

12. Either the boys or their parents _____ driving to the game.
(is, are)

13. Neither ivy nor moss _____ here.
(grows, grow)

Personal Narrative

In a **personal narrative**, the writer tells about a personal experience. A personal narrative is autobiographical, but it typically focuses on a specific event.
A personal narrative
• is written in the first-person point of view.
• usually reveals the writer's feelings.
• has a beginning, a middle, and an end.

DIRECTIONS > **Read the personal narrative below. Then answer the questions that follow.**

The family birthday party began as usual. First, my family gathered after dinner with my presents. I was excited, but I thought I knew what I was getting. My parents had never been able to surprise me.

After I had opened one gift, I heard a faint rustling noise. I paused for a moment, but I heard nothing more. A minute later, I noticed that a large box moved! It was creepy! I jumped to my feet in alarm.

Laughing, my father then picked up the moving present. The box had no bottom at all. A fluffy white kitten was curled up where the present had been. I was finally surprised—with the best birthday present I had ever received.

1. From what point of view is this narrative told?

   _____

   What words are clues to this point of view?

   _____

2. How did the writer feel at the beginning of the narrative?

   _____

3. How did the writer's feelings change by the end of the narrative?

   _____

4. List the events of the narrative in the order in which they happened. Write a signal word or phrase if one is given for each event.

   a. _____

   b. _____

   c. _____

   d. _____

   e. _____

Personal Narrative: Proofreading

To be a good proofreader, look for one type of error at a time. For example, proofread once for capitalization errors, once for punctuation errors, and once for spelling errors.

PROOFREADER'S MARKS

≡ Capitalize.
⊙ Add a period.
∧ Add something.
⋏ Add a comma.
∨∨ Add quotation marks.
⤳ Cut something.

⌃ Replace something.
↰ Transpose.
◯ Spell correctly.
⁋ Indent paragraph.
/ Make a lowercase letter.

DIRECTIONS ▷ **Proofread the personal narrative, paying special attention to spelling. Use the Proofreader's Marks to correct at least eight errors.**

What an amazing experience my bothers and I had with the wind last autunm! We had driven with our parents to Point Reyes, north of San francisco. Point Reyes is known as one of the windyest spots in the cuontry, and on that day the winds were raging up to 50 miles an hour all along the California coast.

I had no way of determining the speed of the wind at Point reyes that afternoon. I can only tell you that when we jumped into the air, we were blown a full five feet before landing The wind picked us up and carried us with the force of rushhing water. we simpply could not fall backward. The wind was so strong that we could lean back against it and let it support us as firmly as a brick wall would. My brothers and I decided to take a short walk downwind along the beach. We allowed the wind to push us along at a rappid pace. For a while we stoped walking altogether. We simply jumped into the air, let ourselves be blown along like empty milk cartoons, and landed. Then we jumped into the air again. Borne by the wind, we progressed as quickly as if we had been walking

Personal Narrative: Graphic Organizer

Write a personal narrative about something you do well. Use the graphic organizer to plan your personal narrative.

What are you going to write about?

Tell what your skill is, how you learned it, and when you use it.

Tell how your skill makes your life more interesting.

Personal Narrative: Writing

Tips for Writing a Personal Narrative:
- Write from your point of view. Use the words *I* and *my* to show your readers that this is your story.
- Think about what you want to tell your readers.
- Organize your ideas into a beginning, a middle, and an end.
- Write an interesting introduction that "grabs" your readers.
- Write an ending for your story. Write it from your point of view.

DIRECTIONS Write a personal narrative about something you do well. Use the graphic organizer on page 95 as a guide for writing. Be sure to proofread your writing.

_____

_____

_____

_____

_____

_____

_____

_____

_____

_____

_____

_____

_____

_____

_____

_____

_____

_____

_____

_____

Descriptive Paragraph

A **descriptive paragraph** appeals to the reader's senses of sight, hearing, smell, touch, and taste. In a few words, it paints a picture of a subject.

ⓓ ⓓ

DIRECTIONS ▷ **Read the paragraph. Underline the topic sentence. Then complete the items below.**

The room had clearly been ransacked. The drawers of the dresser next to the window were open and empty. A trail of assorted clothing led to the closet. The closet stood empty, its contents strewn across the bed and the floor. Glass from a broken perfume bottle crunched loudly underfoot, the fragrance of its contents mixing with the smell of garlic. The only item left undisturbed was a portrait on the wall over the bed. Its subject, a solemn young woman, stared thoughtfully into the room, like a silent witness to the recent crime.

1. List at least five words or phrases the writer used to appeal to your senses. After each word or phrase, tell which sense it is: *sight, hearing, smell,* or *touch.*

   _____

   _____

   _____

   _____

   _____

   _____

2. Is this paragraph written in space order or in time order?

   _____

3. What words did the writer use that indicate this type of order?

   _____

Descriptive Paragraph: Proofreading

To be a good proofreader, look for one type of error at a time. For example, proofread once for capitalization errors, once for punctuation errors, and once for spelling errors.

PROOFREADER'S MARKS

≡ Capitalize.
⊙ Add a period.
∧ Add something.
⋏ Add a comma.
ⱽⱽ Add quotation marks.
⤳ Cut something.

⌃ Replace something.
ᴕ Transpose.
○ Spell correctly.
Ⴕ Indent paragraph.
/ Make a lowercase letter.

 **DIRECTIONS** Proofread the description, paying special attention to the capitalization and end punctuation of sentences. Use the Proofreader's Marks to correct at least eight errors.

A set of smooth stone steps led up to a flat clearing in the forest Here the sun's rays filtered down through the branches of the towering pines, and the ground was covered with fragrant green pine needles. the carpet of needles felt thick and soft under Nina's feet.

a gentle breeze rustled the branches Nina inhaled the scent of the pines as it drifted on the breeze. mingled with the scent of pine was the smell of the pale green mosses growing on the north sides of the trees.

What was that in the middle of the clearing Nina saw a large stump, just under three feat tall and a full three feet in diameter. four smaller stumps were arranged around it Paul was already seated on one of the smaller stumps, and the large stump was clearly just the right hieght for a table.

On the large stump lay a basket of juicy blackberries, a canteen, and two shiny metal cups Paul looked up at Nina and asked, "Are you ready for a treat?"

Descriptive Paragraph: Proofreading

Descriptive Paragraph: Graphic Organizer

DIRECTIONS To describe something, a writer tells what he or she sees, hears, feels, tastes, and smells. The writer uses interesting words. Describe a favorite relative. Use the graphic organizer to plan your descriptive paragraph. Which relative will you describe? Write his or her name in the circle. Then write words that describe this relative on the lines. Draw a picture of the person.

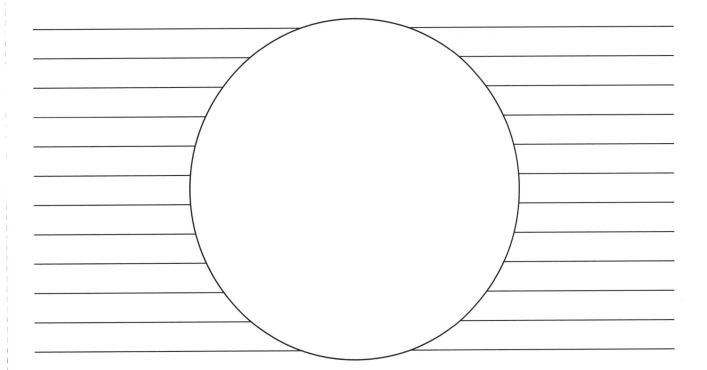

Descriptive Paragraph: Writing

Tips for Writing a Descriptive Paragraph:
• Use your voice when you write. That means you should use your special way of expressing yourself.
• Help readers see, smell, taste, feel, and hear what you are writing about.
• Use interesting words to help you describe.
• Use similes and metaphors to help your readers imagine the experience you are writing about.

DIRECTIONS ▸ Describe a favorite relative. Use the graphic organizer on page 99 as a guide for writing. Be sure to proofread your writing.

_____
_____
_____
_____
_____
_____
_____
_____
_____
_____
_____
_____
_____
_____
_____
_____
_____
_____

How-to Paragraph

A **how-to paragraph**
- tells how to do something.
- has a topic sentence and detail sentences.
- tells what materials to use and what steps to follow.

 **DIRECTIONS** ➤ Use the following sentences to write a how-to paragraph. First, write the topic sentence that gives the purpose of the instructions. Next, write the sentence that lists the needed materials. Then write the steps in correct time order. Put in any special information where it is needed.

Boil the ginger, letting the water evaporate until only one cup of water remains.

You will need a fresh ginger root, three cups of water, a knife, and a glass pot or kettle.

If you ever need to warm your body when you are chilled, you should try making some ginger tea.

First, put three cups of water into the glass pot.

Next, cut six slices of ginger root. The slices should be $\frac{1}{8}$- to $\frac{1}{4}$-inch thick.

Strain the ginger tea into a cup. Drink it hot.

Add the ginger to the water in the pot.

_____

_____

_____

_____

_____

_____

_____

_____

_____

_____

_____

_____

_____

_____

How-to Paragraph: Proofreading

To be a good proofreader, look for one type of error at a time. For example, proofread once for capitalization errors, once for punctuation errors, and once for spelling errors.

PROOFREADER'S MARKS

≡ Capitalize.
⊙ Add a period.
∧ Add something.
⋏ Add a comma.
∨∨ Add quotation marks.
⤴ Cut something.

⌄ Replace something.
⁒ Transpose.
○ Spell correctly.
ꟍ Indent paragraph.
/ Make a lowercase letter.

 **DIRECTIONS** > **Proofread the how-to paragraphs below, paying special attention to commas. Use the Proofreader's Marks to correct at least eight errors.**

With the help of a little tuna fish and some acting skill, you can easily get your dog Titan to take his pill. As you know, Titan often begs for tuna but you never give him any. If you suddenly offer Titan some tuna with the pill inside it, he will become suspicious and refuse eat it. Try this method instead.

Make a small ball of tuna around Titan's pill. Put the tuna ball on a plate. Then find sumthing you like to eat and put that on the plate, too. Take your plate and sit down at the kitchen table.

Titan will probably be watching you carefully but you should ignore him. He's a very smart dog and it will not be easy to fool him. your chances of success are best if you if just pretend you don't see him.

Titan will soon sit beside you, and start to beg. Eat your own food and continue to ignore Titan. Then, very casually, allow the ball of tuna to fall to the floor. You should make a quick grab for the tuna but you must be sure that Titan gets to it first. Titan will eagerly gulp the tuna—and the pill.

How-to Paragraph: Graphic Organizer

 **DIRECTIONS** Think about your favorite park or restaurant. Write a how-to paragraph telling someone how to get there from your house. Use the graphic organizer to help you write.

Writing Plan

Name the place for which you will write directions.

List the streets.

Write the steps someone should follow in order. Number the steps.

Write some sequence words that help the reader know what to do.

How-to Paragraph: Writing

Tips for Writing a How-to Paragraph:
• Choose one thing to teach someone.
• Focus on a plan.
  1. Think of all the materials someone will need.
  2. Think of all the steps someone will follow.
• Use sequence words in your directions.

DIRECTIONS Think about your favorite park or restaurant. Write a how-to paragraph telling someone how to get there from your house. Use the graphic organizer on page 103 as a guide for writing. Be sure to proofread your writing.

_____

_____

_____

_____

_____

_____

_____

_____

_____

_____

_____

_____

_____

_____

_____

_____

_____

_____

_____

Compare and Contrast Paragraph

A **compare and contrast paragraph**
- tells about the similarities and the differences of two or more items.
- answers the same questions about each item.

DIRECTIONS Read each paragraph. Label it *compare* or *contrast*. Circle the names of the two items being compared. Underline the key words that signal similarity or difference.

1.   The new house was similar to the old house in some ways. Like the old house, it had three bedrooms. Both houses had two bathrooms. They both had fireplaces in the living room. The old house had a separate dining room, and so did the new house.

_____

2.   The new house looked and felt different from the old house, and Janet did not know if she liked it as much. The old house was nearly one hundred years old. The new house had just been built. Unlike the old two-story house, the new house was all on one level. The hardwood floors at the old house could be seen beneath the old-fashioned rugs, while wall-to-wall carpet covered the floors of the new house.

_____

DIRECTIONS Use the information in the paragraphs above to complete the chart. Write the different characteristics of each house in the correct column. In the middle column, write the characteristics that both houses share.

Old House	Both	New House
_____	_____	_____
_____	_____	_____
_____	_____	_____
_____	_____	_____

Compare and Contrast Paragraph: Proofreading

To be a good proofreader, look for one type of error at a time. For example, proofread once for capitalization errors, once for punctuation errors, and once for spelling errors.

PROOFREADER'S MARKS

≡ Capitalize.
⊙ Add a period.
∧ Add something.
⋏ Add a comma.
∨∨ Add quotation marks.
↗ Cut something.

⌃ Replace something.
↰ Transpose.
◯ Spell correctly.
⊬ Indent paragraph.
／ Make a lowercase letter.

DIRECTIONS ▷ **Proofread the paragraphs of comparison and contrast, paying special attention to subject-verb agreement. Use the Proofreader's Marks to correct at least seven errors.**

People sometimes asks me who my best friend is. Truthfully, I do not know. I have two close friends, and I like them both very much.

My friends judy and Margie is alike in many ways. Both are intelligent, loyal, and helpful Either can carry on a great conversation. Each has an excellent sense of humor, and we all enjoy many of the same activities.

However, my two friends are different in many ways. I has more arguments with Judy. She complains if she does not like something, and she argue if she disagrees with me. Margie rarely complains or argues, so we almost never fights.

On the other hand, Judy is a more honest friend. She always says exactly what she thinks or feels. In contrast, margie never say anything negative to me about things i have said or done. Instead, she may say something to someone else, and her comments often gets back to me. If Judy has a complaint, she discusses it with the person who has caused the problem.

Compare and Contrast Paragraph: Graphic Organizer

DIRECTIONS Compare and contrast two subjects you study at school. Use the Venn diagram to help you plan your writing. List what is true only about A in the A circle. List what is true only about B in the B circle. List what is true about both A and B where the circles overlap.

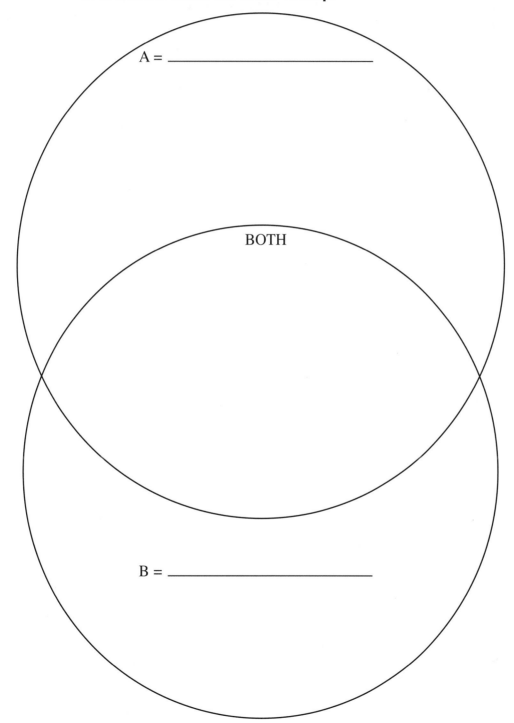

A = _____

BOTH

B = _____

Compare and Contrast Paragraph: Writing

Tips for Writing a Compare and Contrast Paragraph:
- Find information about your subjects.
- Organize the information you find into main ideas.
- Use details to explain each main idea.
- Explain how the subjects are alike.
- Explain how the subjects are different.
- Use your last paragraph to summarize your main ideas in a new way.

DIRECTIONS ▷ Compare and contrast two subjects you study at school. Use the Venn diagram on page 107 as a guide for writing. Be sure to proofread your writing.

Compare and Contrast Paragraph: Writing

Persuasive Letter

A **persuasive letter**
- states an opinion and gives supporting reasons.
- has a topic sentence and detail sentences.
- often has a "clincher" sentence.

DIRECTIONS ➤ Read this business letter. Then answer the questions that follow.

Kensington
London, England
December 21, 1846

Mr. Ebenezer Scrooge
Financial District
London, England

Dear Mr. Scrooge:
   One of your employees, Bob Cratchit, has applied for work with us. Mr. Cratchit is a fine man, and I think you should think carefully before letting him go. First of all, Bob is very quick with numbers—a valuable trait in your type of work. Second, he is a very loyal worker. If it were not for his son, Tiny Tim, he would never think of leaving your firm. Third, Mr. Cratchit is willing to work very long hours for very little pay. I feel I am certain that you should see to this immediately. For some reason, I sense that it may be of great importance.

Sincerely,

James Martin

1. What opinion is stated in this business letter?

   _____

2. Write the topic sentence that states this opinion.

   _____

3. How many reasons does the writer give to support his opinion?

   _____

4. What warning does the writer give?

   _____

Persuasive Letter: Proofreading

To be a good proofreader, look for one type of error at a time. For example, proofread once for capitalization errors, once for punctuation errors, and once for spelling errors.

PROOFREADER'S MARKS

≡ Capitalize.	⌃ Replace something.
⊙ Add a period.	⇌ Transpose.
∧ Add something.	○ Spell correctly.
⋏ Add a comma.	⁋ Indent paragraph.
ⱽⱽ Add quotation marks.	/ Make a lowercase letter.
⚲ Cut something.	

DIRECTIONS ▷ **Proofread the business letter, paying special attention to capitalization and punctuation. Use the Proofreader's Marks to correct at least nine errors.**

431 palm Avenue

Normand Massachusetts 02162

june 26, 2005

Mr. glen Scrubb

Grime-Away cleaners

816 Ruby Street

Normand, massachusetts 02162

dear Mr. Scrubb

My family has used your cleaners for seven years, and your service has always been satisfactory. however, last Thursday I picked up my favorite slacks from Grime-Away and discovered a tear in the cuff. I know that the tear was not there when I brought the slacks to Grime-Away. The clerk said she could not have the tear repaired without your authorization. Please send me a note stating that you will pay four the repair.

Thank you for your help.

sincerely,

Donald Todd

Persuasive Letter: Graphic Organizer

In a persuasive letter, a writer tries to convince someone or a group of people to do something. The writer tries to make the reader feel a certain emotion about the topic he or she writes about.

ⓓ ⓓ

DIRECTIONS ▸ **Write a persuasive letter to the principal of your school asking him or her to change the homework policy of your school. Use this graphic organizer to help you write.**

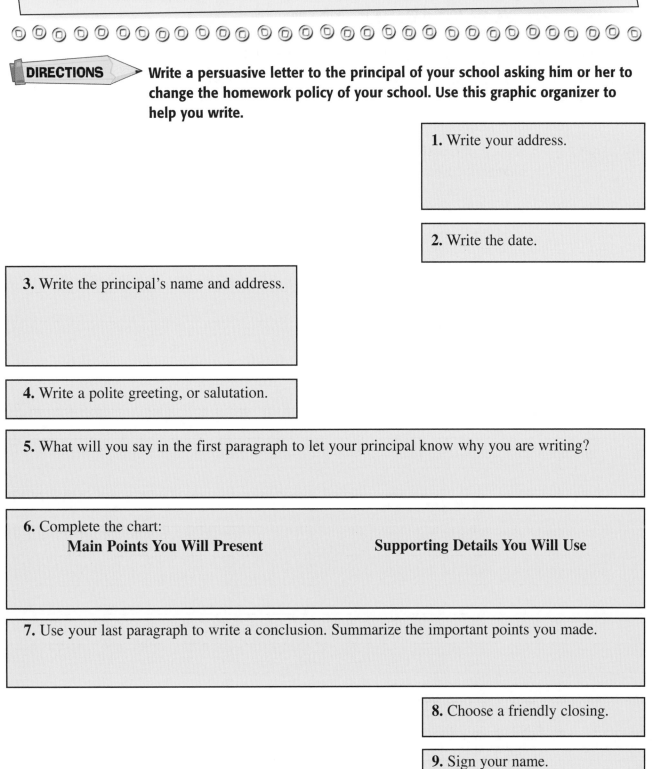

1. Write your address.

2. Write the date.

3. Write the principal's name and address.

4. Write a polite greeting, or salutation.

5. What will you say in the first paragraph to let your principal know why you are writing?

6. Complete the chart:

Main Points You Will Present	Supporting Details You Will Use

7. Use your last paragraph to write a conclusion. Summarize the important points you made.

8. Choose a friendly closing.

9. Sign your name.

Persuasive Letter: Writing

DIRECTIONS ➤ Write a persuasive letter to the principal of your school asking him or her to change the homework policy of your school. Use the graphic organizer on page 111 as a guide for writing. Be sure to proofread your writing.

_____

_____

_____

_____

_____

_____

_____

_____

_____

_____

_____

_____

_____

_____

_____

_____

_____

_____

_____

_____

Persuasive Essay

A **persuasive essay**
• gives an opinion about an issue.
• gives facts and reasons to back up the opinion.
• has an introductory paragraph, supporting paragraphs, and a conclusion.

DIRECTIONS ▷ **Read the following statements from a persuasive essay. Write the word or group of words from the box that best describes the techniques used in the statement.**

testimonial	emotional words	faulty generalization
begging the question	bandwagon technique	

1. We have to keep greedy builders from gobbling up our wilderness to make a buck.

   _____

2. Jack Tenor, the famous athlete, says that they passed a similar law in his town and everyone is happy with it.

   _____

3. Join the thousands of people all over the country who are demanding laws to restrict building in their area.

   _____

4. Since my neighbors like my idea, we're sure that this is what the community wants.

   _____

5. If you are a good citizen, of course you will support this law.

   _____

6. Do not trade the unspoiled beauty and the restful peace of our country for the crowded, smoggy rat race of the city.

   _____

7. María Gómez, a university professor, says that life in the city can be difficult.

   _____

Persuasive Essay: Proofreading

To be a good proofreader, look for one type of error at a time. For example, proofread once for capitalization errors, once for punctuation errors, and once for spelling errors.

PROOFREADER'S MARKS

≡ Capitalize.

⊙ Add a period.

∧ Add something.

⩗ Add a comma.

⩔⩔ Add quotation marks.

✄ Cut something.

⌃ Replace something.

⤮ Transpose.

◯ Spell correctly.

¶ Indent paragraph.

/ Make a lowercase letter.

 **DIRECTIONS** > **Proofread this persuasive essay, paying special attention to capitalization of proper nouns. Use the Proofreader's Marks to correct at least nine errors.**

The people of the World are faced with alarming environmental problems. I am convinced that we must all cooperate through international agencys to solve these problems. Working alone, one state or one nation cannot protect its land and people from environmental hazards. The problems faced by people in the united states are also problems for people in canada, Japan, and russia. Only by facing these problems together and trying to work out cooperative solutions can we protect ourselves and our Planet.

There are several reasons why international cooperation is needed. in the first place, some environmental dangers threaten the whole plant rather than local areas. Damage to the ozone layer is a good example. If someone in nebraska uses an aerosol spray, the chemicals do not stay in Nebraska. Those damaging chemicals travel to the ozone layer, where they affect the whole world. Therefore, a State or Country cannot protect itself against ozone damage simply by passing a law forbidding the local use of aerosols.

Persuasive Essay: Graphic Organizer

Should sodas and candy be sold in vending machines on school campuses? Write a persuasive essay expressing your opinion. Use the graphic organizer to help you write.

What will the topic of your essay be?	What is your opinion on this topic?
_____	_____
_____	_____

Reason 1	Why? Support your reason.
_____	_____
_____	_____
_____	_____
_____	_____
	_____

Reason 2	Why? Support your reason.
_____	_____
_____	_____
_____	_____
_____	_____
	_____

Reason 3	Why? Support your reason.
_____	_____
_____	_____
_____	_____
_____	_____

Persuasive Essay: Writing

Tips for Writing a Persuasive Essay:
- Grab your reader's attention in the first paragraph.
- State your opinion clearly.
- Support your opinion with clear examples.
- Present your examples from least important to most important.
- Use the last paragraph to summarize your essay.
- Use your last paragraph to leave the reader convinced you are right.

DIRECTIONS Should sodas and candy be sold in vending machines on school campuses? Write a persuasive essay expressing your opinion. Use the graphic organizer on page 115 as a guide for writing. Be sure to proofread your writing.

Poem

A **poem**
- expresses feelings, often through description.
- presents vivid images.
- may or may not rhyme.

DIRECTIONS > Read each stanza of this poem. Answer the questions that follow.

The Sea That Joins the World

I stand at the blue, wave-ruffled border of the Pacific
And my eyes follow it to a distant meeting with the sky.
My mind tries to follow abroad to far-off continents
That Australians, Japanese, and Russians occupy.

My body sinks in the frothing salty ocean,
A bathtub shared with tribes in distant lands.
I feel my arms extend to unknown peoples
And, through the ocean, touch them with my hands.

1. What does the title suggest about the poem?

   _____

2. What picture is created in the first line?

   _____

   _____

3. Does this poem contain rhyme? If so, which words rhyme?

   _____

4. What metaphor does the second stanza contain?

   _____

5. What feeling is expressed in the second stanza?

   _____

Poem: Proofreading

To be a good proofreader, look for one type of error at a time. For example, proofread once for capitalization errors, once for punctuation errors, and once for spelling errors.

PROOFREADER'S MARKS

≡ Capitalize.	⌐ Replace something.
⊙ Add a period.	⁔ Transpose.
∧ Add something.	◯ Spell correctly.
⩑ Add a comma.	¶ Indent paragraph.
ⱽⱽ Add quotation marks.	/ Make a lowercase letter.
⤵ Cut something.	

 **DIRECTIONS** ▷ **Proofread the poem, paying special attention to the correct use of pronouns. Use the Proofreader's Marks to correct at least seven errors.**

My Fair-Weather Friend

My greatest admirer is mine shadow.

He admires me so much that he mimics everything myse

He follows me everywhere.

I drag him threw puddles as i walk around.

His glides over their surface like a black film of oil.

I drag him over logs and stones.

He slithers over they like a snake.

I bump him into Boulders and Buildings.

He stays by me side, obedient as a slave, faithful as a fair-weather friend.

"What?" you ask. "I always thought a fair-weather friend was unfaithful."

Exactly. My shadow deserts me as soon as the son goes down or the sky turns gray.

He will not follow I into dark rooms or deep caves.

He is only a fair-weather friend.

Poem: Graphic Organizer

Poetry is usually written in rhythmic lines rather than in sentences. In a **rhymed** poem, syllable sounds are repeated at the ends of paired lines. For example, the following poem follows a rhyme scheme, or pattern. The first and third lines rhyme, and the second and fourth lines rhyme.

Example:

>A sleeping fawn,
>A single crow—
>Above, the dawn,
>Still night below.

In **unrhymed** poetry, rhythm, figurative language, and imagery express a mood.

Example:

>The quiet night
>Gentle breathing of branches.
>The sun creeps
>Glinting edges of hilltops.
>A crow calls
>Shrill salute to the morning.

DIRECTIONS Think about your favorite holiday. Write colorful words that describe it on the graphic organizer. Then use the graphic organizer to help you write a poem about your favorite holiday.

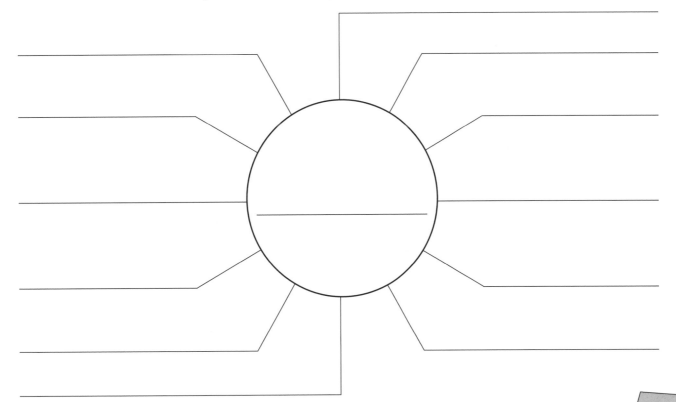

Poem: Writing

DIRECTIONS Write a poem about your favorite holiday. Use the graphic organizer on page 119 as a guide to help you write. Be sure to proofread your writing.

_____

_____

_____

_____

_____

_____

_____

_____

_____

_____

_____

_____

_____

_____

_____

_____

_____

_____

_____

_____

Writing for a Test

Writing for a test requires special skills. Usually, the writer has no choice of topic; the topic is assigned. Often, there is a time limit during which all stages of the writing process must be carried out. Keeping in mind any such restrictions, you should build in the time to plan and revise your writing. Thinking about these questions may help:

PREWRITING

Choosing a Topic
- What questions must I answer?
- Am I being asked to compare, give an opinion, explain, analyze, or describe?
- What kind of writing will fulfill this assignment?

Gathering Information
- Am I allowed to refer to my textbook?
- Can I make a rough outline to help organize my thoughts?

DRAFTING
- What will I use as my topic sentence?
- How much time do I have to finish the draft? How many minutes should I allot to each question or essay?

RESPONDING AND REVISING
- Have I answered the question completely?
- Are there any additional facts I should include?

PROOFREADING
- Have I spelled every word correctly?
- Are my sentences grammatically correct?

FINAL DRAFT
- Do I have time to rewrite this neatly?

Essay Questions

Many tests include essay questions. The test taker must divide the given time into time to plan, time to draft, and time to revise each answer.
Example:

How did Native Americans adapt to their environment? Give two examples.

Inuit—igloos, travel for food 2 Iroquois—homes of wood and bark, hunted game 1	Freewrite facts and ideas Organize by numbering facts in logical order
Topic sentence: Native Americans had to adapt their housing and eating habits to their environment.	Develop main idea for topic
Native Americans had to adapt their housing and eating habits to their environment. The Iroquois lived in the Eastern forests, where trees and game animals were plentiful. They built houses called longhouses out of wood and bark. An example of adaptation to extreme conditions is the Inuit way of life. In the Arctic, many Inuit built igloos for winter homes. They, too, traveled in search of food.	Write

Tips for Writing for a Test:
• Freewrite facts and ideas.
• Organize by numbering facts in logical order.
• Develop the main idea for a topic.
• Write.

Questions

Writing to Prompts

Many schools use tests to evaluate students' ability to write. One kind of test uses a **writing prompt**, which requires a written response to a statement, a question, or a picture. Careful reading of the prompt will help determine the writing form, the audience (if given), and the purpose for writing (to inform, to persuade, to entertain, or to describe). Often, students are supplied with enough paper to plan and write the response.

Example:

Prompt	**Some people say exercise not only keeps you fit but also can give you more energy and better concentration. Do you agree or disagree? Write an essay in which you state your opinion and support it with at least one example.**
Organizing notes	Does exercise keep me fit, boost my energy, and help me concentrate? Yes. Example of this: my swimming Reasons why (or how?) it helps: 1. the exercise gives me energy 2. easier to concentrate when I've exercised
Thesis statement	Frequent exercise can help improve your energy level and concentration.

⊙⊙⊙⊙⊙⊙⊙⊙⊙⊙⊙⊙⊙⊙⊙⊙⊙⊙⊙⊙⊙⊙⊙⊙⊙⊙⊙⊙⊙⊙⊙⊙⊙⊙⊙⊙⊙

 **DIRECTIONS** ➤ **Choose one of the writing prompts below. Follow the tips on pages 121 and 122 to prepare your written response to the prompt.**

1. People take care of their teeth so they will stay healthy for a lifetime. Think about the steps in your daily dental-care routine. Then, write a how-to paper explaining this process.

2. Have you read a book that has been made into a movie or cartoon? How are they alike? How are they different? Write a paper that compares and contrasts the two versions of the story.

3. Are you allowed to stay up as late as you think you should? What would you like your bedtime to be? Write a letter to convince your parents that you should be able to stay up later.

Parts of a Book

The **title page** tells the name of a book and the author's name. It also tells the name of the company that published the book.

The **copyright page** is on the back of the title page. It tells when the book was published.

The **foreword/preface** contains introductory comments about the book. It can be written by the author or someone else.

The **contents page** lists the titles of the chapters or units in the book and the pages on which they begin.

The **glossary** contains definitions of difficult or unfamiliar words that appear in the book.

The **bibliography** is a list of books about a certain subject. It can also be a list of books the author used or referred to in the text.

The **index** is a list of all the topics in a book. It is in alphabetical order and lists the page or pages on which each topic appears.

DIRECTIONS > Identify in which part of a book the following information can be found. Choose from the list in the box below.

contents page	bibliography	index	title page
foreword/preface	copyright page	glossary	content or body

1. *All Wrapped Up in Mummies*
   By Sandy Desserte
   Impossible Press
   Cleveland, Ohio _____

2. The book you are about to read is the result of more than twenty years of research. To gather information about mummies, Miss Desserte made several trips to Egypt and actually took part in a number of archaeological digs.

   _____

3. Suggested Readings
   Aldred, Cyril. *The Egyptians*. Thames and Hudson, London, 1965.
   Barnes, James. *Land of the Pharaohs*. Jones Publishing Co., London, 1924.

   _____

4. Copyright © 1993 by Sandy Desserte _____

5. Foreword.....................................8
   Looking for Mummies.............................11
   Under the Desert Sky ....22 _____

Parts of a Book, page 2

DIRECTIONS ▷ In which book part would you find answers to these questions? Choose from the list in the box below.

title page   copyright page   contents page

AFRICA	Copyright © 1985 by	CONTENTS
A Land of Empires	Landmark Publications	

AFRICA
A Land of Empires

by
Dorothy J. Morgan

LANDMARK PUBLICATIONS
Chicago   New York   Toronto

Copyright © 1985 by
Landmark Publications
Acknowledgments
Millburn Publishing Company:
  "Watusi Legends" from *African*
  Literature, ed. by R.R. Adams.
  Copyright © 1967.
Tifford, Inc. "Sunset" from
  Poetry Monthly, October 1981.
All rights reserved. Printed in
the United States of America.

CONTENTS
1. The Africa of the Romans ... 1
2. The Sarakole Empire 25
3. The Mali Empire 53
4. The Ethiopian Empire 75
5. The Baguirimi Empire 153
Glossary 175
Index 187

contents page	bibliography	index	title page
foreword/preface	copyright page	glossary	content or body

1. What is the meaning of *papyrus*?
   _____

2. On what page does Chapter 2 begin?
   _____

3. When was the book published?
   _____

4. Who published the book?
   _____

5. What are some other books on the same topic?
   _____

6. Who wrote the book?
   _____

7. Who wrote the introductory remarks?
   _____

8. Which is the shortest chapter?
   _____

DIRECTIONS ▷ List at least one item of information that can be found in each of the following book parts.

9. copyright page _____

10. title page _____

11. foreword or preface _____

12. index _____

13. glossary _____

14. contents page _____

15. bibliography _____

Outlines

An **outline** organizes information into main topics, subtopics, and details. An outline follows certain rules of capitalization and punctuation.

DIRECTIONS ▷ Write *main topic*, *subtopic*, or *detail* to identify each item in this part of an outline.

I. Loch Ness monster _____

   A. Where it lives _____

      1. Northern Scotland _____

      2. Deep, narrow lake _____

   B. What it looks like _____

      1. Small head _____

      2. Long, thin neck _____

      3. Body 90 feet long _____

DIRECTIONS ▷ The lines in this part of the outline are in the correct order. Find the error or errors in each line, and write the line correctly. Remember to indent the lines properly.

II. the Yeti _____

   a. where it lives _____

      1 in Asia _____

      2 in the Himalayas _____

   b. what it looks like _____

      1. large ape or man _____

      2 covered with hair _____

DIRECTIONS ▷ Research famous monsters or other imaginary creatures. On your own paper, write an outline of the information you find. Revise and proofread your work, checking for correct outline form.

Using a Thesaurus

A **thesaurus** is a book that gives synonyms, words that have nearly the same meaning, and antonyms, words that mean the opposite of a word. Many thesauruses are like dictionaries. The entry words are listed in dark print in alphabetical order. Guide words at the top of the page tell which words can be found on the page. Use a thesaurus to enrich your vocabulary and make your writing more colorful.
Example:

buccaneer	budge

buccaneer *syn.* pirate, sea robber, desperado, outlaw, pillager, plunderer, ransacker, looter, raider

DIRECTIONS ➤ Rewrite each sentence. Use a thesaurus to replace the underlined word.

1. The Ross family left their <u>home</u> early.

_____

2. The children climbed into the car <u>eagerly</u>.

_____

3. Bill Ross was a <u>beginning</u> driver.

_____

4. He had just finished a <u>class</u> in driving at school.

_____

5. Bill and his father <u>changed</u> places before they reached the mountains.

_____

_____

6. The <u>smell</u> of pines was everywhere.

_____

7. Bill and Susan immediately went for a <u>walk</u>.

_____

8. They loved to spend time in the <u>woods</u>.

_____

9. A cool <u>wind</u> blew through their hair.

_____

10. They hiked until they were <u>tired</u>.

_____

Using a Dictionary

A **dictionary** lists words in alphabetical order, giving their pronunciation, part of speech, and definition. There are two guide words at the top of every dictionary page. The word on the left is the first word on the page, and the word on the right is the last word. Each word in the dictionary is an entry word.

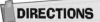 **DIRECTIONS** Read the dictionary entries and answer the questions that follow.

---

nation   nature

na·tion [nā´shən] *n.* **1** A group of people who live in a particular area, have a distinctive way of life, and are organized under a central government. They usually speak the same language. **2** A tribe or federation: the Iroquois *nation.*

na·tion·al [nash´ən·əl] **1** *adj.* Of, belonging to, or having to do with a nation as a whole: A *national* law; a *national* crisis. **2** *n.* a citizen of a nation. **–na´tion·al·ly** *adv.*

na·tion·wide [nā´shən·wīd´] *adj.* Extending throughout or across a nation.

na·tive [nā´tiv] **1** *adj.* Born, grown, or living naturally in a particular area. **2** *n.* A person, plant, or animal native to an area. **3** *n.* One of the original inhabitants of a place; aborigine. **4** *adj.* Related or belonging to a person by birth or place of birth: one's *native* language.

Native American One of or a descendant of the peoples already living in the Western Hemisphere before the first Europeans came.

na·tive-born [nā´tiv·bôrn´] *adj.* Born in the area or country stated: a *native–born* Floridian.

---

1. What part of speech is *nation*? _____

2. What part of speech is *native-born*? _____

3. What is the meaning of *nationwide*? _____

4. What is the base word of *nationally*? _____

5. Which meaning of the word *nation* is used in the following sentence?

   Wilma Mankiller is the first woman to become chief of the Cherokee *nation.*

   _____

6. What is the entry word for *nationally*? _____

7. How many syllables does *nationwide* have? _____

8. Would *natural* be found on the page with the guide words shown above? _____

Using a Computerized Card Catalog

Libraries used to keep track of their inventory by having cards for each book. These cards were alphabetized and kept in "card catalogs." Most libraries now use **computerized card catalogs**. You can look up books by title, author, or subject. The computer can tell you whether the book is available or has been checked out. In public libraries in cities, you can find out which branches have the book if your location doesn't have it. Sometimes you can call another branch and have the book sent to the library closest to you.

DIRECTIONS Refer to the directions inside the box to answer the questions.

To look for a book by the author's last name:		To look for a book by title:	
STEP	**ACTION**	**STEP**	**ACTION**
1	Type: FA	1	Type: FT
2	Type: Author's last name	2	Type: Book title
3	Press: <RETURN> key	3	Press: <RETURN> key

1. Write the three steps you would follow to find a book by Thor Heyerdahl using a computerized book catalog.

   _____

   _____

   _____

2. Write the three steps you would take to find a book called *Treasures of the Deep*.

   _____

   _____

   _____

3. If you type FA to find a book by author's name, and you type FT to find a book by book title, what do you think you would type to find a book by subject? Explain your answer.

   _____

   _____

4. What three steps would you take to find books about whales?

   _____

   _____

   _____

Taking Notes

Taking notes helps you organize information when you do research. Some facts are more important than others. Write down only the main ideas when you take notes.

DIRECTIONS ▷ **Read the following paragraphs and take notes about them on the note cards below.**

Among women in history, Queen Hatshepsut of Egypt holds a special place. She was the only woman ever to rule Egypt with the all-powerful title of pharaoh. Hatshepsut succeeded her husband Thutmose II to the throne about 1504 B.C. She enjoyed a relatively long reign, ruling as pharaoh for 21 years. During that time, Hatshepsut was remarkably productive. Egypt's trade improved under her leadership, and she embarked on a major building program.

NOTES

Meng T'ien, the general in charge of building the Great Wall, is also credited with another, smaller construction project. Sometime before 200 B.C., General T'ien is believed to have invented the *cheng*, a musical instrument of the zither family. Like other zithers of Asia, the *cheng* has a long, slightly curved sound box with strings that stretch the length of the instrument. Frets, or stops, are located on the sound box to help produce the melody. Although the *cheng* is no longer popular in China, its descendants are still popular in other Asian countries. In Vietnam the *tranh* is still used for courtly music, and the *koto* enjoys wide popularity in Japan.

NOTES

Analyzing a Textbook

A textbook gives much information. Use the table of contents to find the facts you need. The glossary defines difficult words in the text.

◎◎◎◎◎◎◎◎◎◎◎◎◎◎◎◎◎◎◎◎◎◎◎◎◎◎◎◎◎◎◎◎◎

DIRECTIONS ▷ Read this table of contents for a science textbook about oceans. Answer the questions that follow.

1. In which chapter would you find information about whales, dolphins, and sea otters? _____

   How do you know? _____

2. In which chapter would you expect to find pictures of the damage caused by an oil slick? _____

   What makes you think so? _____

3. Which is the longest chapter? _____

4. In which chapter might you find out how coral reefs are formed? _____

5. You're interested in finding out what kinds of seaweed grow near the coastlines. Where would you

   look? _____

6. You want to find out what the word *salinity* means. Where might you find it in this book?

   _____

7. In which chapter might you find information about pelicans? _____

8. You want to learn which creatures live in the deepest parts of the ocean. Which chapter would you

   read? _____

9. Which is the shortest chapter? _____

10. In which chapter would you find out what valuable things we can get from the oceans? _____

Using an Encyclopedia

An **encyclopedia** is a set of reference books, each of which is called a **volume**. Each volume contains many articles on various topics. The topics are arranged alphabetically. The spine of each volume indicates which articles are within. For example, a volume that says *N-O* has articles beginning with the letters *N* and *O*. At the end of most articles there is a list of related topics. These topics are called cross-references. Often you can find more pertinent information by reading these articles.

DIRECTIONS > Find the entry for *armadillo* in an encyclopedia. Then answer the following questions.

1. Where do armadillos live? _____

2. What do they eat? _____

3. How do they protect themselves? _____

4. How much do they weigh? _____

5. Which encyclopedia did you use? _____

DIRECTIONS > Find the entry for *Sir Edmund Hillary* in an encyclopedia. Then answer the following questions.

6. Why is Sir Edmund Hillary famous? _____

7. What country was he from? _____

8. When was he born? _____

9. What was his family's business? _____

10. How high is Mount Everest? _____

DIRECTIONS > Find the entry for *Zimbabwe* in an encyclopedia. Then answer the following questions.

11. Where is Zimbabwe located? _____

12. Does it have a coast? _____

13. What is the capital and the largest city? _____

14. What is the former name of Zimbabwe? _____

15. What are the most important agricultural products? _____

Identifying Reference Sources

> **atlas** – a book of maps
> **thesaurus** – a book of synonyms and antonyms
> **dictionary** – gives the pronunciation and the definitions of words
> **almanac** – a book that is published each year and gives facts about various topics
> such as the tides, weather, time the sun rises, etc. Much of the information is
> presented in charts, tables, and graphs. An almanac also presents general information.
> **encyclopedia** – a set of volumes that has articles about various topics
> *Books in Print* – lists books that have been published about various subjects

DIRECTIONS ➤ **Write the reference source in which each item of information can be found. Choose from the list below. There may be more than one correct answer.**

| atlas | almanac | thesaurus | encyclopedia | dictionary | *Books in Print* |

1. **Languages** – It is estimated that there are thousands of languages spoken in the world. Following is a list of the major languages spoken by the greatest number of people. They are ranked in order of usage.

Name of Language	**Major Areas Where Spoken**
Chinese (Mandarin)	China
English (has the most words – 790,000)	U.S., U.K, Canada, Ireland, Australia, New Zealand

   _____

2. **sincere** – honest, truthful, honorable, frank, open, aboveboard, unreserved, veracious, true, candid

   _____

3. **writing** – visible recording of language peculiar to the human species. Writing permits the transmission of ideas over vast distances of time and space and is essential to complex civilization. The first known writing dates from 6000 B.C. . . .

   _____

4. **language** [lang´ gwij] *n.* **1. a.** Spoken or written human speech. *Language* is used to communicate thoughts and feelings. **b.** A particular system of human speech that is shared by the people of a country or another group of people. **2.** Any system of signs, symbols, or gestures used for giving information.

   _____

5. Auberge, Tony, ed. *The Oxford Guide to Word Games*. LC83-25140. 240 p. 1984. 14.95 (ISBN 0-19-214144-9). Oxford U. Pr.

   _____

Using the Internet

You can use a computer to help you do research on the Internet. The World Wide Web allows you to access many websites that have pictures and sounds as well as written information. This makes it an interesting way to do research. Search engines are instruments that help you find the information you want.

DIRECTIONS ▸ Connect to the Internet. Use the search engine www.yahooligans.com to search for the subject *elephant*. Then answer the questions.

1. How many category matches were listed? _____

2. How many site matches were listed? _____

3. Under which category do you find the most resources listed? _____

4. List the website addresses that have pictures of elephants. _____

_____

5. List the website addresses that have magazine articles listed. _____

_____

_____

DIRECTIONS ▸ Use these different search engines to do a search for the subject *elephant*. Then answer the questions.

www.yahooligans.com	www.ajkids.com	www.altavista.com

1. Which search engine gave you the best results? _____

2. Which search engine gave you the most results? _____

3. Which search engine was the easiest to use? _____

4. If you were writing a report on elephants, which search engine would have helped you the most?

_____

5. Pick a topic that interests you, and search the Internet for information. Which search engine(s) did you use? Tell what you find out about your topic. _____

_____

_____

_____

Answer Key

Unit 1

Page 6

1. Carlos—person; week—idea or thing; aunt—person; uncle—person, **2.** daughter—person; Mary—person; cousin—person, **3.** children—person; discussions—thing; happiness—idea, **4.** family—thing; ranch—place or thing; Montana—place, **5.** Saturday—thing; neighbor—person; meal—thing, **6.** Grandma—person; dishes—thing; table—thing, **7.** Sam—person; kitchen—place or thing; dishes—thing, **8.** month—idea or thing; memory—idea or thing; veterans—person; town—place, **9.** Volunteers—person; mural—thing; school—place or thing, **10.** Dr. García—person; mayor—person; parade—thing; bands—thing, **11.** lifeguard—person; days—thing; week—idea or thing, **12.** Lightning—thing; barn—thing or place

Page 7

1. Harriet Tubman was born as a <u>slave</u> in the <u>state</u> of Maryland., **2.** Her <u>husband</u>, John Tubman, was free., **3.** Harriet fled from the <u>plantation</u> of her <u>master</u>., **4.** The former <u>slave</u> found <u>freedom</u> in Philadelphia., **5.** Her <u>family</u> and <u>friends</u> were still enslaved., **6.** This courageous <u>woman</u> returned for her <u>sister</u>, Mary Ann., **7.** Her <u>brother</u>, James, escaped later with his <u>family</u>., **8.** During her <u>life</u>, Harriet led many other <u>escapes</u>.

Page 8

1. painter; school; painting, **2.** name; style; painting, **3.** movement, **4.** artists, **5.** painters, **6.** exhibit; paintings; group, **7.** canvas; eye; light, **8.** painters; way; objects; light, **9.** boat, **10.** painter, **11.** Children; world; hopscotch, **12.** versions; game, **13.** town; children; board; squares, **14.** stone; coin; square; foot; square, **15.** paragraph; sport, **16.** Diego Rivera; Mexico, **17.** Mexico, **18.** Spanish; Mexico, **19.** Zapotec Indians, **20.** Rivera; Mexico City; United States, **21.** Detroit Institute of Arts; Michigan; Diego Rivera, **22.** Constitution; United States; Constitutional Convention, **23.** Philadelphia; Pennsylvania, **24.** Bill of Rights; James Madison, **25.** April; George Washington

Page 9

Common nouns: generals, river, violin, tune, sorrow, song, melody, joy, place, songs, future, country, peace
Proper nouns: General Tang, General Wang, Tang, General Lang, General Mang,
Webs: Nouns That Name People: generals, General Tang, General Wang, General Lang, General Mang
Nouns That Name Ideas: sorrow, joy, future, peace, The additional nouns will vary.

Page 10

1. horses, **2.** donkeys, **3.** patches, **4.** days, **5.** puppies, **6.** porches, **7.** ladies, **8.** dresses, **9.** hills, **10.** trails

Page 11

1. women, **2.** Cars, **3.** oxen; calves, **4.** sheep, **5.** Wolves, **6.** teeth; knives, **7.** potatoes, **8.** tomatoes, **9.** Deer; leaves

Page 12

1. brushes, **2.** louse, **3.** butterfly, **4.** men, **5.** suitcase, **6.** turkeys, **7.** watch, **8.** melodies, **9.** cheese, **10.** gas, **11.** cranberries, **12.** scarves, **13.** heroes, **14.** axes, **15.** blueberry, **16.** goose, **17.** mouths, **18.** reefs, **19.** canaries, **20.** glitch, **21.** umbrella, **22.** well, **23.** vases, **24.** moss, **25.** lances, **26.** masses, **27.** patches, **28.** videos, **29.** babies, **30.** gulches, **31.** cellos, **32.** sashes

Page 13

1. Lewis Carroll's book, **2.** the knife's edge, **3.** the book's cover, **4.** Mayor Sanita's speech, **5.** the flowers' aroma, **6.** the children's bicycle, **7.** the sirens' roar, **8.** the rainbow's colors, **9.** Chris's shoes, **10.** the women's purses, **11.–15.** Answers will vary.

Page 14

1. sculptor's, **2.** artist's, **3.** hour's, **4.** country's, **5.** thief's, **6.** Robert Frost's, **7.** week's, **8.** minute's, **9.** weaver's, **10.** Samuel Clemens's, **11.** wolf's, **12.** nurse's, **13.** King Henry's, **14.** moment's, **15.** secretary's, **16.** Mr. Jones's, **17.** hostesses', **18.** teachers', **19.** women's, **20.** masters', **21.** workers', **22.** hours', **23.** oxen's, **24.** spies', **25.** buffaloes', **26.** surgeons', **27.** sheep's, **28.** secretaries', **29.** Britain's worst balloonist, **30.** a colleague's help, **31.** the balloon's ropes, **32.** the flyers' calls for help

Page 15

1. Luis's—singular, **2.** children's—plural, **3.** parents'—plural, **4.** sheep's—plural, **5.** deer's—plural, **6.** cousins'—plural, **7.** person's—singular, **8.** adults'—plural; children's—plural, **9.** Wilsons'—plural, **10.** Uncle Bernie's—singular, **11.** neighbor's—singular, **12.** families'—plural

Page 16

1. they—stories, **2.** his—Aesop, **3.** he—slave, **4.** it—story, **5.** its—donkey, **6.** she—owner, **7.** The owner gave the dog a soft bed and fed it well., **8.** The donkey tried to make its owner treat it well., **9.** The donkey learned that it should not try to be something else., **10.** Can you write two fables and illustrate them?, **11.** The chief engineer and her/his team watched., **12.** Moses took a kite and attached a rope to it.

Page 17

1. his; Thurgood Marshall, 2. their; parents, 3. her; mother, 4. he; Marshall, 5. It; Howard University Law School, 6. her, 7. her, 8. his, 9. him, 10. they

Page 18

1. us—object pronoun, 2. me—object pronoun, 3. She—subject pronoun, 4. She—subject pronoun, 5. her—object pronoun, 6. we—subject pronoun, 7. He—subject pronoun, 8. us—object pronoun, 9. her—object pronoun, 10. me—object pronoun, 11. him—object pronoun, 12. you—subject pronoun, 13. I—subject pronoun, 14. They—subject pronoun, 15. him—object pronoun

Page 19

1. I, 2. We, 3. her, 4. They, 5. them, 6. him, 7. they, 8. them, 9. I, 10. We, 11. I, 12. They, 13. him, 14. her, 15. them, Sentences will vary. Be sure that two of the following pronouns are used correctly: me, us, she, he.

Page 20

1. Annie Oakley was famous for her shooting ability., 2. Mr. Oakley let her use his gun., 3. Buffalo Bill made Annie a star in his show., 4. Annie never missed her target., 5. Audiences could hardly believe their eyes., 6. Jeremy wants to use your stereo., 7. The dog devoured its food., 8. The Reynas had their couch reupholstered., 9. I want to change my schedule., 10. The animals ran for their lives.

Page 21

Answers may vary. Possible answers are given. 1. their, 2. our, 3. his, 4. our, 5. their, 6. its, 7. their, 8. theirs, 9. their, 10. their, 11. her, 12. its, 13. their, 14. his, 15. their, 16. their, 17. Its

Page 22

1. herself—Diane, 2. himself—Ben, 3. themselves—members, 4. ourselves—we, 5. myself—I, 6. yourself—you, 7. itself—dog, 8. themselves—Ed and Beverly, 9. myself—I, 10. ourselves—Estella and I, 11. herself, 12. itself, 13. himself, 14. yourself, 15. ourselves, 16. themselves, 17. myself, 18. ourselves, 19. yourself, 20. themselves

Page 23

1. Everyone—singular, 2. Some—plural, 3. Everything—singular, 4. anybody—singular, 5. many—plural, 6. have, 7. create, 8. helps, 9. needs, 10. want, 11. is

Page 24

1. Who, 2. Whom, 3. who, 4. whom, 5. Who, 6. whom, 7. who, 8. Who, 9. whom, 10. Who, 11. Who's, 12. Whose, 13. Who's, 14. Who's, 15. whose, 16. Whose, 17. Who's, 18. Who's, 19. whose, 20. who's

Page 25

1. him; some; her, 2. him, 3. She; them, 4. few, 5. I; them, 6. her, 7. He; it, 8. I, 9. they; her, 10. him, 11. herself, 12. it, 13. them; herself; she; her, 14. her, 15. themselves, 16. they; her, 17. she; it, 18. their, 19. herself, 20. she, 21. their, 22. her; hers, 23. herself; she, 24. her, 25. he, 26. themselves, 27. it, 28. she, 29. she; herself, 30. she; it, 31. me; I; them, 32. I; he; it, 33. she, 34. I; her; I, 35. I; myself

Page 26

1. an—article; enormous—describing, 2. long—describing; cold—describing, 3. Rich—describing; the—article; black—describing; fertile—describing, 4. the—article; early—describing, 5. The—article; a—article; sociable—describing, 6. A—article; calm—describing; alert—describing; smallest—describing, 7. important—describing; an—article; early—describing, 8. Nightly—describing; rich—describing

Page 27

Answers will vary.

Page 28

1. African; Africa, 2. Hungarian; Hungary, 3. English; England, 4. Yugoslavian; Yugoslavia, 5. Italian; Italy, 6. Tibetan; Tibet, 7. Islamic; Islam, 8. Egyptian; Egypt, 9. Japanese; Japan, 10. Mexican; Mexico, 11.–15. Sentences will vary. Be sure that proper adjectives are used correctly.

Page 29

1. This—singular, 2. those—plural, 3. These—plural, 4. these—plural, 5. that—singular, 6. this—singular, 7.–14. Sentences will vary. 7. pronoun, 8. adjective, 9. pronoun, 10. adjective, 11. pronoun, 12. adjective, 13. pronoun, 14. adjective

Page 30

1. warm—air, 2. sweet—flowers, 3. High—sun, 4. peaceful—horses, 5. happy—Sharon, 6. eager—She, 7. ready—horse, 8. beautiful—day, 9. skillful—surgeon, 10. bitter—mango, 11. fast—horse, 12. gray—coat, 13. silver—it, 14. unusual—Horses, 15. well-trained—They, 16. brave—Rin Tin Tin/Lassie, 17. good—they, 18. fearless—Rin Tin Tin, 19.–20. Sentences will vary.

Page 31

1. colder; coldest, 2. safer; safest, 3. funnier; funniest, 4. flatter; flattest, 5. shinier; shiniest, 6. taller; tallest, 7. whiter; whitest, 8. sweeter; sweetest, 9. sadder; saddest, 10. younger; youngest, 11. larger, 12. smaller, 13. smallest

Page 32

Answers may also use *less* and *least*. 1. more energetic; most energetic, 2. more difficult; most difficult, 3. more generous; most generous, 4. more affectionate; most affectionate, **5.** more active; most active, **6.** worse; worst, **7.** more; most, **8.** more likely; most likely, **9.** more expensive; most expensive, **10.** more crowded; most crowded, **11.** Ruffles is the most beautiful puppy of the litter., **12.** Sport is more intelligent than Ruffles., **13.** Of all the puppies, Tuffy is the most fun.

Page 33
1. stronger; more impressive, **2.** most elaborate, **3.** beautiful; greatest, **4.** more aggressive; largest, **5.** best, **6.** bad, **7.** better, **8.** better; worse, **9.** more, **10.** best, **11.** The; fierce, **12.** This; the; first; the, **13.** Few; Union, **14.** A; the; Confederate, **15.** The; heavy, **16.** That; an, **17.** Many; both, **18.** a; pivotal; American, **19.** the; several, **20.** a; memorable; the

Page 34
1. originated, **2.** compete, **3.** leaped, **4.** stretched, **5.** grabbed, **6.** dribbled, **7.** aimed, **8.** flew, **9.** bounced, **10.** jumped, **11.–15.** Sentences will vary.

Page 35
1. celebrated—action, **2.** is—linking, **3.** reaches—action, **4.** cooked—action, **5.** appeared—linking, **6.** greeted—action, **7.** smelled—linking, **8.** became—linking, **9.** looked—linking, **10.** is—linking, **11.** rises—action, **12.** escapes—action, **13.** are—linking, **14.** were—linking, **15.** was—linking, **16.** study—action, **17.** recycles—action, **18.** was—linking, **19.** opened—action, **20.** were—linking

Page 36
Action verbs: compete, need, carries, defeated, ran, ran
Linking verbs: are, are, is, is, is, **1.–10.** Answers will vary.

Page 37
1. are moving—moving, **2.** have lived—lived, **3.** am missing—missing, **4.** has been—been, **5.** had moved—moved, **6.** do want—want, **7.** has accepted—accepted, **8.** is living—living, **9.** was working—working, **10.** did offer—offer, **11.** Does like—like, **12.** was complaining—complaining, **13.** had lived—lived, **14.** is enjoying—enjoying, **15.** will find—find, **16.** has entered—entered, **17.** might meet—meet, **18.** may visit—visit, **19.** is living—living, **20.** could give—give

Page 38
1. helping, **2.** helping, **3.** main, **4.** main, **5.** main, **6.** helping, **7.** main, **8.** helping, **9.** helping, **10.** main, **11.** main, **12.** helping, **13.** helping, **14.** helping, **15.** helping, **16.–20.** Answers will vary. Suggested: **16.** are blooming, **17.** will be, **18.** should visit, **19.** does; need, **20.** were; picked

Page 39
1. studies—present, **2.** reading—present participle, **3.** taught—past participle, **4.** learned—past participle, **5.** visited—past, **6.** gone—past participle, **7.** seen—past participle, **8.** read—past participle, **9.** planning—present participle, **10.** talks—present, **11.** learns—present, **12.** watching—present participle

Page 40
2. trying; tried; tried, **3.** showing; showed; shown, **4.** talking; talked; talked, **5.** bringing; brought; brought, **6.** ringing; rang; rung, **7.** creating; created; created, **8.** flying; flew; flown, **9.** drinking; drank; drunk, **10.** witnessing; witnessed; witnessed, **11.** wearing; wore; worn, **12.** catching; caught; caught, **13.** growing; grew; grown, **14.** beginning; began; begun, **15.** going; went; gone, **16.** sitting; sat; sat, **17.** thinking; thought; thought, **18.** seeing; saw; seen, **19.** teaching; taught; taught, **20.** understanding; understood; understood, **21.** forgetting; forgot; forgotten, **22.** splashing; splashed; splashed, **23.** eating; ate; eaten, **24.** watching; watched; watched, **25.** arriving; arrived; arrived

Page 41
1. works—present, **2.** prepared—past, **3.** will set—future, **4.** planted—past, **5.** will appear—future, **6.** will pick—future, **7.** pulls—present, **8.** will be—future, **9.** will bat—future, **10.** bats—present, **11.** played—past, **12.** changes—present, **13.** gives—present, **14.–17.** Sentences will vary. **14.** waters, **15.** will dig, **16.** will grow, **17.** helped

Page 42
1. have started—present perfect, **2.** will have discussed—future perfect, **3.** had suggested—past perfect, **4.** have enjoyed—present perfect, **5.** will have finished—future perfect, **6.** has written—present perfect, **7.** had interviewed—past perfect, **8.** have chosen—present perfect, **9.** has enjoyed, **10.** had met, **11.** will have known, **12.** have shared, **13.** had recommended

Page 43
1. am, **2.** have, **3.** Are, **4.** Does, **5.** were, **6.** are, **7.** was, **8.** are, **9.** do, **10.** have, **11.–14.** Answers may vary. Suggested: **11.** was, **12.** had, **13.** is, **14.** Does

Page 44
1. grown, **2.** bought, **3.** sold, **4.** spent, **5.** taken, **6.** become, **7.** seen, **8.** given, **9.** eaten, **10.** froze, **11.** made, **12.** chosen, **13.** told, **14.** grew, **15.** bought

Page 45
1. North America, **2.** travel, **3.** continents, **4.** route, **5.** canal, **6.** rumble, **7.** noise, **8.** forests, **9.** people, **10.** homes, **11.** tomatoes, **12.** potatoes, **13.** covers, **14.** pillows, **15.** nap, **16.–19.** Sentences will vary. Suggested: **16.** Rough seas near Cape Horn endangered the ships., **17.** Ships can carry passengers from one ocean to another in far less time., **18.** A Panama Canal pilot guides ships through the Canal., **19.** The United States paid money to Panama for control of the Canal.

Page 46

1. Sheila told Don a secret., **2.** Don gave her his promise of silence., **3.** Mr. Miller was giving Ryan a surprise party., **4.** He had sent Sheila an invitation., **5.** Mrs. Miller handed Don an invitation., **6.** Don asked Mrs. Miller a question., **7.** guests, **8.** friends, **9.** me, **10.** us, **11.** her, **12.** me, **13.** me, **14.** family, **15.** them, **16.** everyone

Page 47

1. hiker, **2.** member, **3.** friend, **4.** walker, **5.** Michelle, **6.** girl, **7.** climber, **8.** teacher, **9.** part, **10.** portrait, **11.** artist, **12.** test, **13.** judge, **14.** Estella, **15.** poodle, **16.–19.** Sentences will vary.

Page 48

1. went—intransitive, **2.** had visited—transitive, **3.** drove—transitive, **4.** drove—intransitive, **5.** rode—intransitive, **6.** saw—transitive, **7.** felt—intransitive, **8.** loved—transitive, **9.** did stop—intransitive, **10.** had found—transitive, **11.** had built—transitive, **12.** inherited—transitive, **13.** sat—intransitive, **14.** drove—intransitive, **15.** would see—transitive, **16.** offered—transitive, **17.** gave—transitive, **18.** entered—transitive, **19.** bristled—intransitive, **20.** gave—transitive, **21.** gave—transitive, **22.** understood—transitive

Page 49

1. early—when, **2.** up—where, **3.** very—to what extent, **4.** lazily—how, **5.** cautiously—how, **6.** warmly—how, **7.** outside—where, **8.** happily—how, **9.** quite—to what extent, **10.** tonight—when, **11.** very—quietly: adverb; quietly—watched: verb, **12.** quite—still: adjective, **13.** gradually—awoke: verb, **14.** sweetly—greeted: verb, **15.** reluctantly—returned: verb, **16.** suddenly—felt: verb; very—hungry: adjective

Page 50

1. Very—no, **2.** rather—no, **3.** Recklessly—yes, **4.** Suddenly—yes, **5.** desperately—yes, **6.** later—yes, **7.** quite—no, **8.** sternly—yes, **9.** always—yes, **10.** quite—no, **11.–14.** Sentences will vary. Be sure that each sentence includes the adverb and that the position of adverbs in sentences is varied.

Page 51

1. lower; lowest, **2.** nearer; nearest, **3.** more slowly; most slowly, **4.** more seriously; most seriously, **5.** more eagerly; most eagerly, **6.** faster; fastest, **7.** more frequently; most frequently, **8.** more readily; most readily, **9.** more noticeably; most noticeably, **10.** easier; easiest, **11.** more often, **12.** highest, **13.** more carefully, **14.** more accurately, **15.** farther, **16.** More slowly

Page 52

1. ever, **2.** no, **3.** Nowhere, **4.** no, **5.** anybody, **6.** everything, **7.** Neither, **8.–10.** Sentences will vary.

Page 53

1. seriously, **2.** well, **3.** really, **4.** shortly, **5.** immediately, **6.** stubbornly, **7.** quickly, **8.** fiercely, **9.** bravely, **10.** good, **11.** powerful, **12.** perfectly, **13.** cruelly

Page 54

The words in bold should be circled. **1.** in 1271, **2.** with them, **3.** beyond the eastern **mountains**, **4.** to **China**, **5.** for many **years**, **6.** from **China**, **7.** about it, **8.** through **Asia**, **9.** for his **readers**, **10.** about **Asia**; from Marco Polo's **book**, **11.** over the railing, **12.** for England, **13.** to the passengers, **14.** down the gangplank, **15.** into the Atlantic Ocean

Page 55

1. of ice; Sheets, **2.** below the ice; land, **3.** with dog sleds; Explorers, **4.** from the United States; admiral, **5.** on Ross Ice Shelf; camp, **6.** from the boat; view, **7.** of water; spouts, **8.** in the boat; people, **9.** in the world; mammals, **10.** of the porpoises; trainer, **11.** in the crowd; people, **12.** of each show; beginning, **13.** into the air; leaps, **14.** for the performers; rewards, **15.** of Earth's surface; percent, **16.** of that water; percent, **17.** of the water; rest, **18.** on Earth; ocean

Page 56

1. with enthusiasm—supported: verb, **2.** against the English king—spoke: verb, **3.** on foot—traveled: verb, **4.** from his home—far: adverb, **5.** about freedom—enthusiastic: adjective, **6.** on Earth—live: verb, **7.** in the ocean—swim: verb, **8.** with great intelligence—behave: verb, **9.** through its lungs—breathe: verb, **10.** for long periods—can dive: verb, **11.** beneath the ocean's surface—work: verb, **12.** in small diving ships—descend: verb, **13.** in a moment—would crush: verb, **14.** for quick maneuvers—are designed: verb, **15.** to the ocean floor—carry: verb

Page 57

1. into, **2.** different from, **3.** between, **4.** into, **5.** among, **6.** in, **7.** could have, **8.** among, **9.** between

Unit 2

Page 58

1. sentence, **2.** not a sentence, **3.** sentence, **4.** not a sentence, **5.** sentence, **6.** not a sentence, **7.** sentence, **8.** sentence, **9.** not a sentence, **10.** sentence, **11.** not a sentence, **12.** not a sentence, **13.** sentence, **14.** not a sentence, **15.–19.** Answers will vary.

Page 59

1. imperative; period, **2.** exclamatory; exclamation point, **3.** declarative; period, **4.** interrogative; question mark, **5.** declarative; period, **6.** interrogative; question mark, **7.** declarative; period, **8.** interrogative; question mark, **9.–10.** Sentences may vary. Suggested: **9.** Watch that ape., **10.** Is it copying my movements?

Page 60

1. <u>Amelia Bloomer</u> <u>did not invent bloomers</u>., **2.** <u>Bloomers were the first slacks for women</u>., **3.** <u>These pants</u> <u>were very loose and comfortable</u>., **4.** <u>Elizabeth Smith Miller</u> <u>became tired of long skirts and petticoats</u>., **5.** <u>She</u> <u>first wore the pants in public</u>., **6.** <u>The new outfit</u> <u>was described in Amelia Bloomer's newspaper</u>., **7.** <u>People</u> <u>began to call the pants "bloomers."</u>, **8.** <u>Most people</u> <u>were shocked to see women in pants</u>., **9.** <u>The circus</u> <u>began with a parade</u>., **10.** <u>Every performer</u> <u>wore a glittery costume</u>., **11.** <u>Lillie</u> <u>had been to the circus twice</u>., **12.** <u>The acrobats</u> <u>flew through the air</u>., **13.** <u>Our gym teacher</u> <u>has taught us to tumble</u>., **14.** <u>The children</u> <u>bought refreshments</u>., **15.** <u>The audience</u> <u>saw the animals perform</u>., **16.** <u>Her aunt</u> <u>took her to the circus</u>., **17.** <u>The work</u> <u>is dangerous</u>., **18.** <u>Paolo</u> <u>tore his new red shirt</u>., **19.** <u>The clowns</u> <u>threw candy into the crowd</u>., **20.** <u>The family</u> <u>sat close to the top</u>., **21.–22.** Sentences will vary. 21. subject, 22. predicate

Page 61

1. My best <u>friend</u>, **2.** Some <u>snakes</u>, **3.** <u>Glands</u> in the snake's head, **4.** Special <u>fangs</u>, **5.** The deadly <u>venom</u>, **6.** My <u>brothers</u>, **7.** <u>Jaime</u>, **8.** The <u>contents</u> of that letter, **9.** Two <u>classmates</u> of mine, **10.** This <u>secret</u>, **11.** Several <u>members</u> of the crew, **12.** <u>Angelina</u>, **13.** Many <u>costumes</u>, **14.** Other <u>outfits</u>, **15.** Four <u>students</u>, **16.–18.** Answers will vary.

Page 62

1. <u>carried</u> his board toward the water, **2.** <u>paddled</u> out toward the large breakers, **3.** <u>crashed</u> over his head, **4.** <u>tossed</u> the board into the air, **5.** <u>says</u> nothing to me, **6.** <u>was revealed</u> on Saturday afternoon, **7.** <u>arrived</u> on my birthday, **8.** <u>came</u>, **9.** <u>had</u> a wonderful, fantastic party, **10.** <u>bounced</u> onto the floor, **11.** <u>stared</u> at the eraser for five minutes, **12.** <u>stretched</u>, **13.** <u>bumped</u> into the teacher's desk, **14.** <u>watched</u> the eraser with amazement, **15.** quickly <u>picked</u> it up

Page 63

1. neighbors—interrogative, **2.** woman—declarative, **3.** she—interrogative, **4.** you—interrogative, **5.** article—declarative, **6.** children—interrogative, **7.** boy—declarative, **8.** puppy—declarative, **9.** puppy—exclamatory, **10.** (You)—imperative

Page 64

The words in bold should be circled. **1.** A <u>tornado</u> **or** a <u>hurricane</u>, **2.** <u>Lightning</u> **and** the <u>force</u> of wind, **3.** A <u>person</u>, a large <u>animal</u>, **or** an <u>automobile</u>, **4.** My <u>aunt</u>, my <u>uncle</u>, **and** my younger <u>cousin</u>, **5.** Dark <u>clouds</u> **and** powerful <u>winds</u>, **6.** My <u>aunt</u> **and** <u>uncle</u>, **7.** The <u>family</u>, the <u>cat</u>, **and** the <u>dog</u>, **8.** Their <u>house</u> **and** <u>garage</u>, **9.** The <u>school</u> **and** the <u>house</u> across the street

Page 65

The words in bold should be circled. **1.** <u>flashed</u> for a few minutes **and** then <u>turned</u> red, **2.** <u>slowed</u> **and** finally <u>stopped</u>, **3.** <u>reached</u> over **and** <u>adjusted</u> the radio, **4.** <u>reported</u> on traffic conditions **and** <u>advised</u> drivers, **5.** <u>heard</u> the report **and** <u>chose</u> a different route, **6.** <u>whispered</u>, <u>pointed</u>, **and** <u>made</u> notes, **7.** <u>walked</u> **or** <u>drove</u> across the dusty moonscape during the three and a half years of moon landings, **8.** <u>took</u> soil samples, <u>measured</u> temperatures, **and** <u>tested</u> the lunar gravity, **9.** <u>released</u> the lunar module **and** <u>measured</u> the vibrations from its impact, **10.** <u>brought</u> the mission to a close **and** <u>marked</u> the end of manned moon landings

Page 66

1. compound subject, **2.** compound sentence, **3.** compound predicate, **4.** compound sentence, **5.** compound subject, **6.** compound predicate, **7.** compound subject, **8.** compound sentence, **9.** compound sentence, **10.** compound subject, **11.** compound predicate, **12.** compound sentence, **13.** compound subject, **14.** compound sentence, **15.** compound subject, **16.** compound sentence

Page 67

The words in bold should be circled. **1.** <u>Florence Nightingale was the daughter of an English squire</u>, **but** <u>she was born in Florence, Italy</u>., **2.** She was <u>raised</u> **and** <u>educated</u> in Derbyshire, England., **3.** Florence did not want to be <u>idle</u> **or** <u>useless</u>., **4.** <u>Nursing was not considered a proper occupation for ladies</u>, **but** <u>Florence was determined to be a nurse</u>., **5.** Florence <u>went to Germany</u> **and** <u>studied nursing</u>., **6.** <u>Llamas are quite gentle</u>, **and** <u>people often make pets of them</u>., **7.** Llamas <u>climb easily over rocky terrain</u> **and** <u>make good pack animals in the mountains</u>., **8.** A llama <u>is not carnivorous</u> **and** <u>prefers grass and leaves as food</u>., **9.** <u>Sandra</u> **and** <u>Larry</u> have a pet llama., **10.** <u>Llamas emit a humming sound</u>, **and** <u>you can hear it</u>., **11.** The llama <u>lacks speech organs</u> **and** <u>is mute</u>., **12.** <u>Sally talked to one expert</u>, **and** <u>he told her something interesting</u>., **13.** An angry llama <u>will pull its ears back</u> **and** <u>spit</u>., **14.** <u>Grasses</u> **and** <u>leaves</u> are a llama's main source of food., **15.** Llamas <u>enjoy human company</u> **and** <u>are quite affectionate</u>., **16.** Florence returned to London and became the supervisor of a hospital., **17.** England entered the war, and Florence joined the War Office as a nurse.

Page 68

1. Say—mild, **2.** Hooray—strong, **3.** Well—mild, **4.** Wow—strong, **5.** Hey—strong, **6.–10.** Sentences will vary. Suggested: **6.** Aha! That's the way to pitch., **7.** Oops! She missed that one., **8.** Oh, she'll hit it next time., **9.** Hooray! What a hit she made!, **10.** Wow! Look at her go!, Sentences will vary.

Page 69

1. sentence, **2.** sentence fragment, **3.** sentence, **4.** sentence fragment, **5.** run-on sentence, **6.** sentence fragment, **7.** sentence fragment, **8.** sentence, **9.** run-on sentence, **10.** sentence fragment, **11.–13.** Sentences will vary.

Page 70

Sentences will vary.

Page 71

Paragraphs will vary. Suggested:

      I should begin by telling you how long I have been a customer of Ronnie's. I have shopped at Ronnie's for five years. I have always been satisfied with your merchandise and your service.

      I am happy to have an opportunity to tell you how much I have enjoyed shopping at Ronnie's. However, my letter has a different purpose. I want to ask you to carry my favorite line of sporting goods, Sporty's. I have begun shopping elsewhere for sporting goods. I would rather be shopping at Ronnie's because it is my favorite store. Besides, your other customers would enjoy Sporty's top-quality goods available at Ronnie's low prices.

      Please consider my suggestion. Let me know what you decide.

Page 72

1. clause, **2.** phrase, **3.** phrase, **4.** clause, **5.** phrase, **6.** clause, **7.** phrase, **8.** phrase, **9.** clause, **10.** clause, **11.** clause, **12.** phrase, **13.** clause, **14.–17.** Sentences will vary.

Page 73

1. <u>Cleopatra lived in ancient Egypt,</u> <u>which she ruled</u>.; which, **2.** <u>She ruled with her brother</u> <u>until he seized the throne</u>.; until, **3.** <u>She regained her throne</u> <u>because Julius Caesar helped her</u>.; because, **4.** <u>Mark Antony ruled Rome</u> <u>after Caesar died</u>.; after, **5.** <u>Antony went to Egypt,</u> <u>where he lived for several years</u>.; where, **6.** <u>Antony and Cleopatra died</u> <u>when a Roman army attacked Egypt</u>.; when, **7.** <u>If you go to New York City,</u> <u>consider a visit to Brooklyn</u>.; If, **8.** <u>Fifteen teenagers there gained some fame</u> <u>because they were pollution fighters</u>.; because, **9.** <u>They called themselves the Toxic Avengers,</u> <u>a name borrowed from a pollution-fighting superhero</u>.; a, **10.** <u>Although it was located next to a school,</u> <u>the Radiac Research Corporation was storing large amounts of medical waste</u>.; Although, **11.** <u>When the Toxic Avengers heard about this,</u> <u>they planned a response</u>.; When, **12.** <u>When a crowd gathered for a public rally,</u> <u>the teens told the people about Radiac</u>.; When, **13.** <u>Public awareness grew</u> <u>after the rally was held</u>.; after, **14.** <u>Billy fell in the sewer on a neighborhood street</u> <u>as he was playing on a Saturday afternoon</u>.; as

Page 74

1. compound, **2.** complex, **3.** complex, **4.** compound, **5.** complex, **6.** complex, **7.** compound, **8.** complex, **9.** compound, **10.** complex

Unit 3

Page 75

1. Have you ever lost your voice?, **2.** What a strange feeling that is!, **3.** You try to talk, but you can only squeak., **4.** No one can understand you., **5.** The climbers left their base camp at six in the morning., **6.** Mr. Enami is a train engineer., **7.** Miles found his math problems to be very challenging., **8.** Does the community softball league meet every Friday?, **9.** Pedro and I go to the museum in California., **10.** He is such a conscientious student!

Page 76

Commas and semicolons should be placed after words as listed. **1.** runway, **2.** paper, cardboard, **3.** unloaded, sorted, **4.** her, **5.** gear, **6.** Greek, Latin, **7.** Hey, **8.** agree, **9.** Noah, Carrie, **10.** Dallas, Phoenix, **11.** worse; **12.** pilot, copilot, **13.** Oh, **14.** captain; **15.** great, **16.** low,

Page 77

1. Beth Ann Drake, **2.** President Lincoln, **3.** Central Bookstore, **4.** Waco, Texas, **5.** Logan, Utah, **6.** Italian marble, **7.** me, myself, and I, **8.** English accent, **9.** Union army, **10.** American citizen, **11.** Adams Middle School, **12.** *Beauty and the Beast*, **13.** Latin Club, **14.** Amelia Earhart Boulevard, **15.** Declaration of Independence, **16.** Yellowstone National Park, **17.** Mexican pottery, **18.** New Year's Day

Page 78

1. lb., **2.** oz., **3.** ft., **4.** yd., **5.** ME, **6.** mg, **7.** l, **8.** cc, **9.** USPS, **10.** NBA, **11.** Rodeo Dr., **12.** Old Post Rd., **13.** Fifth Ave., **14.** NCAA, **15.** M.D., **16.** mph, **17.** rpm, **18.** F, **19.** C, **20.** Best Carpet Cleaners, Inc., **21.** The Farley Farragut Co., **22.** Dr. Thomas F. Gorman

Page 79

Joe Bob's Restaurant: Answers will vary.
Student Information Card: School: The Parker School, Address: 120 Grant Ave., Ponca City, OK, Principal: Helena M. Ramírez, First Day of School: Sept. 4, 2005

Page 80

1. *Around the World in Eighty Days*, **2.** *The Pirates of Penzance*, **3.** *Profiles in Courage*, **4.** *Stalking the Wild Asparagus*, **5.** *The Cat Ate My Gymsuit*, **6.** "Shake, Rattle, and Roll", **7.** "Twist and Shout", **8.** "Me and My Shadow", **9.** *The Red Balloon*, **10.** *The Wizard of Oz*, **11.** *Stand by Me*, **12.** "The Body", **13.** *Cujo, Christine, Carrie*, **14.** "Stand by Me", **15.** *Time*, **16.** *Travels with Charley*, **17.** "Welcome to Pittsburgh," **18.** *Monday Night Football*, **19.** *Gorillas in the Mist*

Page 81

1. Leon dragged the huge crate through and shouted, "I'm home, Mom!", **2.** "She isn't back yet," Leon's brother told him., **3.** "Oh, Leon," said his brother, staring at the box, "what is that?", **4.** "Queen Elizabeth I ruled a great empire," Marcia said., **5.** She told her critics, "I have the heart and stomach of a king.", **6.** "Who else had a great impact on a country?" asked Terri., **7.** "Well," Ben remarked, "Mohandas Gandhi inspired a nonviolent revolution in India.", **8.** "Gandhi inspired Martin Luther King!" Terri added., **9.** "New York has a new program," Nancy said, "for student ticket buyers."

Page 82
The words in bold should be circled. **1.** The **company**, <u>High Flyers</u>, forgot to include instructions., **2.** The **Eagle**, <u>our only car</u>, would not start., **3.** Our **neighbor**, <u>Jim Delgado</u>, came to help., **4.** Even **Jim**, <u>a good mechanic</u>, could not start it., **5.** The **starter**, <u>an electric motor</u>, was not working., **6.** The **pilot**, <u>Captain Songrossi</u>, said to fasten our seat belts., **7.** A **prairie**, <u>a kind of grassland</u>, is home to many kinds of plants and animals., **8.** Our **teacher**, <u>Ms. Pesek</u>, does not agree., **9.** Our **store**, <u>Video Visions</u>, has many unusual movies., **10.** The **film**, <u>an exciting dinosaur story</u>, is filed with other adventure films., **11.–12.** Sentence will vary.

Page 83
1. I'd; I would, **2.** I've; I have, **3.** she's; she is, **4.** isn't; is not, **5.** We've; We have, **6.** They've; They have, **7.** I'm; I am, **8.** aren't; are not, **9.** didn't; did not, **10.** They'd; They would, **11.** wasn't; was not, **12.** haven't; have not, **13.** You've; You have, **14.** can't; can not, **15.** Doesn't; Does not, **16.–20.** Sentences will vary. **16.** shouldn't, **17.** won't, **18.** he'd, **19.** let's, **20.** you're

Unit 4

Page 84
Answers will vary. Suggested: **1.** sick, **2.** started, **3.** early, **4.** test, **5.** back, **6.** no one, **7.** left, **8.** noisy, **9.** arrived, **10.** begin, **11.** easy, **12.** right, **13.–18.** Answers will vary. Suggested: **13.** untamed; tame, **14.** daring; timid, **15.** bulky; thin, **16.** lucky; unfortunate, **17.** fix; break, **18.** collect; scatter

Page 85
1. gentle, **2.** pulled tight, **3.** a group of ships, **4.** cracked into pieces, **5.** air; heir, **6.** rode; road, **7.** thrown; throne, **8.** side; sighed

Page 86
1. <u>in</u>active—not active, **2.** <u>im</u>polite—not polite, **3.** <u>pre</u>judge—judge before, **4.** <u>un</u>usual—not usual, **5.** <u>over</u>confident—having too much confidence, **6.** <u>post</u>election—coming after an election, **7.** <u>in</u>expensive—not expensive, **8.** <u>re</u>count—count again

Page 87
1. thoughtful; ful, **2.** grayish; ish, **3.** rainy; y, **4.** restless; less, **5.** harmful; ful, **6.–23.** Answers will vary. Suggested: attendant, attendance, attention, boxer, celebrant, celebration, contestant, competitor, competition, cyclist, determinant, determination, developer, development, dominance, domination, excellence, organizer, organization, perfection, prominence, reverence, salutation, skier

Page 88
1. great-uncle, **2.** three-bedroom, **3.** mountain range, **4.** Everyone, **5.** cuckoo clock, **6.** sunset, **7.** seaweed, **8.** jellyfish, **9.** starfish, **10.** blue-green, **11.** sea lion, **12.** palm trees, **13.** fast-sinking, **14.** three-fourths, **15.** beachfront, **16.** spellbound, **17.** inner tube, **18.** newspaper, **19.** jack-of-all-trades, **20.** earring, **21.–24.** Answers will vary.

Page 89
1. antique, **2.** young, **3.** cozy, **4.** unhurried, **5.** simple, **6.** rare, **7.** Blackened, **8.** sip, **9.** tough, **10.** greasy, **11.** crumbly, **12.** soggy, **13.** loud, **14.** inferno

Page 90
Dialogue will vary. Idioms: the cat got your tongue; hold your horses; knock your socks off; get off my back; on pins and needles; keep my nose to the grindstone; take off; get on the ball; about to burst; Lend me a hand

Page 91
1. holds, **2.** selects, **3.** presents, **4.** travel, **5.** follow, **6.** hear, **7.** ignore, **8.** elect, **9.** affect, **10.** votes, **11.** fail, **12.** share, **13.** has, **14.** hurls, **15.** hits

Page 92
1. like, **2.** are, **3.** is, **4.** provide, **5.** discourage, **6.** frighten, **7.** outruns, **8.** fly, **9.** fights, **10.** change, **11.** hides, **12.** are, **13.** grows

Unit 5

Page 93
1. first person; my, I, me, **2.** excited, but not expecting to be surprised, **3.** The writer became surprised., **4. a.** The family gathered after dinner.—first, **b.** The writer heard a rustling noise.—after, **c.** The writer noticed that a box moved.—a minute later, **d.** Father picked up the present.—then, **e.** The writer was surprised.—finally

Page 94
Errors are corrected in bold type.

What an amazing experience my **brothers** and I had with the wind last **autumn**! We had driven with our parents to Point Reyes, north of San **Francisco**. Point Reyes is known as one of the **windiest** spots in the **country**, and on that day the winds were raging up to 50 miles an hour all along the California coast.

I had no way of determining the speed of the wind at

Point **Reyes** that afternoon. I can only tell you that when we jumped into the air, we were blown a full five feet before landing**.** The wind picked us up and carried us with the force of **rushing** water. **We simply** could not fall backward. The wind was so strong that we could lean back against it and let it support us as firmly as a brick wall would.

[paragraph ident] My brothers and I decided to take a short walk downwind along the beach. We allowed the wind to push us along at a **rapid** pace. For a while we **stopped** walking altogether. We simply jumped into the air, let ourselves be blown along like empty milk **cartons,** and landed. Then we jumped into the air again. Borne by the wind, we progressed as quickly as if we had been walking**.**

Pages 95–96
Graphic organizers and personal narratives will vary.

Page 97
Topic sentence: The room had clearly been ransacked.,
1. Suggested answers: open and empty drawers, strewn clothes, empty closet, portrait of a solemn young woman—all sight; crunch of glass—hearing; fragrance of perfume, garlic smell—smell; broken glass underfoot—touch,
2. space order, **3.** Suggested answers are "next to," "trail . . . led," "underfoot," "on the wall."

Page 98
Errors are corrected in bold type.

A set of smooth stone steps led up to a flat clearing in the forest**.** Here the sun's rays filtered down through the branches of the towering pines, and the ground was covered with fragrant green pine needles. **The** carpet of needles felt thick and soft under Nina's feet.

A gentle breeze rustled the branches**.** Nina inhaled the scent of the pines as it drifted on the breeze. **Mingled** with the scent of pine was the smell of the pale green mosses growing on the north sides of the trees.
[paragraph indent] What was that in the middle of the clearing**?** Nina saw a large stump, just under three **feet** tall and a full three feet in diameter. **Four** smaller stumps were arranged around it**.** Paul was already seated on one of the smaller stumps, and the large stump was clearly just the right **height** for a table.

On the large stump lay a basket of juicy blackberries, a canteen, and two shiny metal cups**.** Paul looked up at Nina and asked, "Are you ready for a treat?"

Pages 99–100
Graphic organizers and descriptive paragraphs will vary.

Page 101
If you ever need to warm your body when you are chilled, you should try making some ginger tea. You will need a fresh ginger root, three cups of water, a knife, and a glass pot or kettle. First, put three cups of water into the glass pot. Next, cut six slices of ginger root. The slices should be $\frac{1}{8}$- to

$\frac{1}{4}$-inch thick. Add the ginger to the water in the pot. Boil the ginger, letting the water evaporate until only one cup of water remains. Strain the ginger tea into a cup. Drink it hot.

Page 102
Errors are corrected in bold type.

With the help of a little tuna fish and some acting skill, you can easily get your dog Titan to take his pill. As you know, Titan often begs for tuna**,** but you never give him any. If you suddenly offer Titan some tuna with the pill inside it, he will become suspicious and refuse **to** eat it. Try this method instead.

Make a small ball of tuna around Titan's pill. Put the tuna ball on a plate. Then find **something** you like to eat and put that on the plate, too. Take your plate and sit down at the kitchen table.

Titan will probably be watching you carefully**,** but you should ignore him. He's a very smart dog**,** and it will not be easy to fool him. **Your** chances of success are best if you [delete extra if] just pretend you don't see him.
[paragraph indent] Titan will soon sit beside you [delete comma] and start to beg. Eat your own food and continue to ignore Titan. Then, very casually, allow the ball of tuna to fall to the floor. You should make a quick grab for the tuna**,** but you must be sure that Titan gets to it first. Titan will eagerly gulp the tuna—and the pill.

Pages 103–104
Graphic organizers and how-to paragraphs will vary.

Page 105
1. Circle: new house, old house; Underline: similar to, Like, Both, both, and so did—compare, **2.** Circle: new house, old house; Underline: different, Unlike, while—contrast. Old House: old, hardwood floor, rugs, two-story; Both: three bedrooms, two bathrooms, fireplace in living room, dining room; New House: brand new, wall-to-wall carpet, one-story

Page 106
Errors are corrected in bold type.

People sometimes **ask** me who my best friend is. Truthfully, I do not know. I have two close friends, and I like them both very much.

My friends **Judy** and Margie **are** alike in many ways. Both are intelligent, loyal, and helpful**.** Either can carry on a great conversation. Each has an excellent sense of humor, and we all enjoy many of the same activities.

However, my two friends are different in many ways. I **have** more arguments with Judy. She complains if she does not like something, and she **argues** if she disagrees with me. Margie rarely complains or argues, so we almost never **fight**.

On the other hand, Judy is a more honest friend. She always says exactly what she thinks or feels. In contrast, **Margie** never **says** anything negative to me about things **I** have said or done. Instead, she may say something to someone else, and her comments often **get** back to me. If Judy has a complaint, she discusses it with the person who has caused the problem.

pages 107–108
Venn diagrams and compare and contrast paragraphs will vary.

Page 109
1. that Bob Cratchit is a good worker, **2.** Mr. Cratchit is a fine man, and I think you should think carefully before letting him go., **3.** 3, **4.** that it may be of great importance

Page 110
Errors are corrected in bold type.

431 **Palm** Avenue
Normand**,** Massachusetts 02162
June 26, 2005

Mr. **Glen** Scrubb
Grime-Away **Cleaners**
816 Ruby Street
Normand, **Massachusetts** 02162

Dear Mr. Scrubb**:**

My family has used your cleaners for seven years, and your service has always been satisfactory. **However**, last Thursday I picked up my favorite slacks from Grime-Away and discovered a tear in the cuff. I know that the tear was not there when I brought the slacks to Grime-Away. The clerk said she could not have the tear repaired without your authorization. Please send me a note stating that you will pay **for** the repair.

Thank you for your help.

Sincerely,
Donald Todd

Pages 111–112
Graphic organizers and persuasive paragraphs will vary.

Page 113
1. emotional words, **2.** testimonial, **3.** bandwagon technique, **4.** faulty generalization, **5.** begging the question, **6.** emotional words, **7.** testimonial

Page 114
Errors are corrected in bold type.

The people of the **world** are faced with alarming environmental problems. I am convinced that we must all cooperate through international **agencies** to solve these problems. Working alone, one state or one nation cannot protect its land and people from environmental hazards. The problems faced by people in the **United States** are also problems for people in **Canada**, Japan, and **Russia**. Only by facing these problems together and trying to work out cooperative solutions can we protect ourselves and our **planet**.

There are several reasons why international cooperation is needed. **In** the first place, some environmental dangers threaten the whole **planet** rather than local areas. Damage to the ozone layer is a good example. If someone in **Nebraska** uses an aerosol spray, the chemicals do not stay in Nebraska. Those damaging chemicals travel to the ozone layer, where they affect the whole world. Therefore, a **state** or **country** cannot protect itself against ozone damage simply by passing a law forbidding the local use of aerosols.

Pages 115–116
Graphic organizers and persuasive essays will vary.

Page 117
Answers will vary. Suggested: **1.** It will focus on the fact that the sea touches every continent., **2.** a view of the coast as the ruffled border of something blue, perhaps fabric, **3.** yes; sky, occupy; lands, hands, **4.** The ocean is compared to a bathtub., **5.** a sense of community formed by bathing in the same ocean

Page 118
Errors are corrected in bold type.

My Fair-Weather Friend
My greatest admirer is **my** shadow.
He admires me so much that he mimics everything **I** do.
He follows me everywhere.
I drag him **through** puddles as **I** walk around.
He glides over their surface like a black film of oil.
I drag him over logs and stones.
He slithers over **them** like a snake.
I bump him into **boulders** and **buildings**.
He stays by **my** side, obedient as a slave, faithful as a fair-
    weather friend.
"What?" you ask. "I always thought a fair-weather friend
    was unfaithful."
Exactly. My shadow deserts me as soon as the **sun** goes
    down or the sky turns gray.
He will not follow **me** into dark rooms or deep caves.
He is only a fair-weather friend.

Pages 119–120
Graphic organizers and poems will vary.

Page 123
Responses to prompts will vary.

Unit 6
Page 124
1. title page, **2.** foreword/preface, **3.** bibliography, **4.** copyright page, **5.** contents page

Page 125
1. glossary, **2.** contents page, **3.** copyright page, **4.** title page, **5.** bibliography, **6.** title page, **7.** foreword/preface, **8.** contents page, **9.–15.** Responses will vary: Suggested:

9. the date a book was published, **10.** title and author of book; publisher, where published, **11.** introductory comments about the book, **12.** list of all the topics in the book and the page numbers where they appear in the book, **13.** definitions of difficult or unfamiliar words that appear in the book, **14.** chapter titles; page numbers on which chapters begin, **15.** other books on the same topic

Page 126

I. main topic, **A.** subtopic, **1.** detail, **2.** detail, **B.** subtopic, **1.** detail, **2.** detail, **3.** detail,

II. The Yeti
    A. Where it lives
        1. In Asia
        2. In the Himalayas
    B. What it looks like
        1. Large ape or man
        2. Covered with hair
Outlines will vary.

Page 127

Answers will vary.

Page 128

1. noun, **2.** adjective, **3.** Extending throughout or across a nation, **4.** nation, **5.** A tribe or federation, **6.** national, **7.** 3, **8.** yes

Page 129

1. 1. Type: FA 2. Type: Heyerdahl 3. Press: <Return> key, **2.** 1. Type: FT 2. Type: Treasures of the Deep 3. Press: <Return> key, **3.** Type FS, because FA means Find Author, and FT means Find Title, so FS means Find Subject., **4.** 1. Type: FS 2. Type: whales 3. Press: <Return> key

Page 130

Notes should include key ideas. Suggested responses: Queen Hatshepsut: Only woman pharaoh. Succeeded Thutmose II about 1504 B.C. Ruled 21 years. Productive: Trade improved. Major building program.

Cheng: Meng T'ien, inventor, before 200 B.C. Musical instrument, zither family. Long, curved sound box. Strings stretch length of box. Frets help produce melody. Descendants of *cheng*: *tranh* (Vietnam); *koto* (Japan)

Page 131

1. Chapter 4; These animals are mammals., **2.** Chapter 7; "Our Oceans in Danger" suggests pollution., **3.** Chapter 4, **4.** Chapter 2, **5.** Chapter 1, **6.** Glossary, **7.** Chapter 5, **8.** Chapter 3, **9.** Chapter 7, **10.** Chapter 6

Page 132

Answers may vary depending on encyclopedia used. **1.** From Argentina north to south central and south eastern parts of the United States, **2.** snails, insects, spiders, and earthworms, **3.** They hide in their burrows if these are close by; if not, they dig a hole. Sometimes they roll up in a ball., **4.** Up to 15 pounds, **5.** Answers will vary., **6.** He and Tenzing Norkay were the first climbers to reach the summit of Mount Everest., **7.** New Zealand, **8.** July 29, 1919, **9.** Beekeeping, **10.** 29,028 ft., **11.** Southern Africa, **12.** No, **13.** Harare, **14.** Rhodesia, **15.** Cattle, coffee, corn, cotton, sugar, tea, tobacco, and wheat

Page 133

1. almanac or encyclopedia, **2.** thesaurus, **3.** encyclopedia, **4.** dictionary, **5.** *Books in Print*

Page 134

Answers will vary.